Eleanor Wilner

Reversing the Spell

NEW AND SELECT??? ???'S

COPPER CANYON PRESS

The publication of this book was supported by grants from the Lannan Foundation, the National Endowment for the Arts, and the Washington State Arts Commission, and by contributions from Elliott Bay Book Company, James Laughlin, and the members of the Friends of Copper Canyon Press.

Library of Congress Cataloging-in-Publication Data
Wilner, Eleanor.
Reversing the spell: new and selected poems / Eleanor Wilner
p. cm.
ISBN 1-55659-082-2 (pbk.)
I. Title.
PS3573.I45673448   1998   97-33927

COPPER CANYON PRESS
P.O. BOX 271, PORT TOWNSEND, WASHINGTON 98368

This book is for Bob, who carries our compass
and for my two Gertrudes

Contents

UP AGAINST IT: NEW POEMS 1993–1996

I. *What Goes On*

II. *The Cohort*

from SHEKHINAH (1984)

I.

II.

from MAYA (1979)

I.

II.

Acknowledgments

With thanks to the editors of the following magazines and anthologies in which these poems in *Up Against It* first appeared:

Beloit Poetry Journal (Chapbook 22): "Abstraction"
Boulevard: "Sunflowers, Repossessed," "Middle-Class Vantage," "On Ethnic Definitions," "Working the Block"
Crab Orchard Review: "Judgment," " '...Zero at the Bone' "
DoubleTake: "Winged Victory"
Johns Hopkins Magazine: "Up Against It"
Kenyon Review: "Of a Sun She Can Remember"
Marlboro Review: "Ode to Innocence"
Michigan Quarterly: "All the Wide Grin of Him," " '...now I can go on and on' "
Northeast Corridor: "What Was Going On," "Blessing"
Philadelphia Inquirer: "Killing the Grubs"
PN Review (England): "Salute to Donald Davie"
Prairie Schooner: "Women Talking," "The Messenger," "Poem of Exile," "Facing into It," "The Pillar"
Southern Review: "*Trümmerfrauen*," "Dinner Party," "You, Failed Pronoun"
Sycamore Review: "Job's Wife, a Twentieth-Century Casting Script"

"Facing into It" was reprinted in *The 1997 Pushcart Prize* XXI: *Best of the Small Presses*

Other poems in this volume are excerpted from the following books: *maya*, the 1979 Juniper Prize selection of the University of Massachusetts Press; *Shekhinah* (1984), *Sarah's Choice* (1989), and *Otherwise* (1993), published by the Phoenix Poets Series, University of Chicago Press, to whom the author expresses her gratitude.

With thanks to the John D. and Catherine T. MacArthur Foundation for the blessed anonymity of its munificence.

For her sumptuous hospitality and for bringing her elegant Italian to the translation of some of these poems, *grazie* to Eleonora Chiavetta. And, for help in the compilation of this manuscript, all thanks to Marcia Pelletiere, for the touchstone and the laughs.

Reversing the Spell

UP AGAINST IT

New Poems 1993–1996

1. *What Goes On*

Trümmerfrauen

(The Rubble-Women)

1. △

In the old paintings, the ones with silken oils
whose vistas opened like a long hall to the eye;
the Virgin with her glowing skin, the child
in her arms, formed a perfect triangle – the art
historians always made a point of that: God
in Euclid's arms, the blue satin shawl and
temporary flesh fit in the pyramid of faith
exactly: abstract and equilateral; the baby held
in her painted lap, fattened for sacrifice;
while in the streets, blood ran, and skinny dogs
prowled the greasy cobblestones; monthly,
the women wore, then washed the red-stained
rags, and the candles in the church flickered
under the bloodless Lady with her lovely face,
under the nailed-up man, the body's long disgrace
impaled naked on the crossroads of the grid.

2. ▲

Outside the ruined church and the bombed
museum, the rubble piles stand along the road;
at the apex of each one, a woman sits, whatever
the weather, and with a little hammer breaks

the mortar from the broken stones. The women
atop the pyramids of rubble tap and tap, the sound
is like the ghostly tapping of woodpeckers in
the burned and blackened place the forest stood.

Behind each of these widow women on her heap
slowly rise the piles of finished stone. Here and there,
little fires still break out, a flurry of fiery ash, lines
of smoke unwinding the flat gray sky.

It is hard to tell the mortar from crushed bones:
a fine sift of gray wants to hang in the air
and to coat the hair of the women
who seem at times almost stone themselves

except for the sound of tapping and the way
the pile behind them grows, clean stone
ready for the mason, the architects
of a future that none of them can bear
to conceive – alone as they are, and cold.

But the relentless percussion of life goes on,
the little hammers rise and fall, descendents
of Thor, of Luther, whose hammers split
the Northern sky, the Christian world –

persistent, they tap and tap, the old mortar
flakes away like a fine snow of stone.
And what can be made of the altars now,
the broken walls of the fallen hearths,
when so much of the future has gone?

Elsewhere, no doubt, men are drawing up
their plans. Out here, the women sit,
each on her pile of stones, their hammers
never stop: tap tap, tap tap, tap tap.

Abstraction

They came that morning, in gowns of pale green and white,
sliding through the slim trees like slants of an unsparing light;

they were noiseless in their coming, and faceless,
except for their eyes, and behind them came a noise,

a clinking, light touch of steel on steel, wind chimes
in the corridors of bone; it followed them, the sound,

as a wake follows a ship, that ruffled disturbance
of what had been even and seamless, a placid

surface, so unperturbed in being what it was.
And when they came, as a wave parts, everything fled

before them, had fled hours, days, before they came,
having sensed their coming from a long way off,

the way snakes know before the seismographs
that the earth will move, and even the mountains

will break, slide in great sheets of mud and rubble,
and swallow the valleys, the inhabited hollows

whose houses were crammed with the unsuspecting,
living like dogs in the dumb incomprehension

of the habitual. The morning was torn where they came,
riven between the slim trees, which were rooted

and could not flee from their own forest nature
like the birds and the insects, the raccoons, opossums,

deer, and the rodents, who had vanished before, leaving
only the stillness behind, and the tension of waiting

which kept even the leaves from stirring, and the wind
held its breath, fearing that the least movement would

shatter the leaves like glass. Every space that once
was the passage for air and light, and the small scurry

of squirrels, became a wound as they entered there,
a legion in the gowns of their office. They were

the priests of postponement, their gifts were subtraction,
pain, and extension of days. They had their rituals,

their instruments, their secret language and passwords;
the forest was not their home, and they had never

heard its secret language, for it always fell silent before
them, and what they came to was only a vacant

room, like the shell of a village that had fled at the news
of an army approaching. And from the edge of the scene,

so composed, and so silent, except for the strange clink
clink of the steel, the trees so straight in their dark lines,

the trunks an abstract study in stripes, rows of harsh light
between them, the figures gliding into the foreground –

from vision's periphery, something begins
to seep, slowly at first, like the oozing of sap from a tree,

and then faster, until it is pouring, a tide of red flooding
out from the edges of vision and swallowing what might

have been, covering whatever it was that was hiding
out there, everywhere, since they came to the forest

whose spirit, a fugitive,
unprovisioned and naked, had fled.

All the Wide Grin of Him

is hovering in the air, there, in the highest
branches, like the fading crescent moon,
tipped in that odd way of what's waning:
a crooked smile, God's grin, the Cheshire
Cat in Wonderland – the smile outlasting
the cat. It fades but refuses to go, hanging
like the pall of ash and smoke over a city
for weeks after the bomb. On a billboard
above Times Square, the man in the Camel ad
has a hole for a mouth, and smoke
puffs out, little o's dissolving like Cheerios
in a bowl of milk.
           Grennian, Anglo-Saxon
root of grin: to show the teeth, to snarl.
Grendel mutters, turns in his long sleep.
The lake has eaten back the boats, the Lady
has withdrawn her arm – sword and all,
and Arthur, all the wide grin of him,
royal jester at the last, his skull
grinning up from a snarl of weeds,
mirror image of the cat-grin above, drowned
moon, or a trick of reflection: the lake
staring back, wearing tradition's bony grin.

While high in the willows, in a tangle
of branches, the wide smile of the Cheshire
Cat, bright as a Japanese lantern, still swings
in the tree with the wind, and the wind chimes
tinkle their sparkle of tunes, and tomorrow
sleeps like a kitten, curled in time's side,
soft, unsuspecting, milk rimming its grin.

Sunflowers, Repossessed

Dreaming, we turn the gods into such shapes
as lead us on, as in the Ramayana
the warrior Mareech turned himself
into a golden deer to lure the lovely Sita
into a demon's arms. Sita, the fragrant one,
moved in a dream of flowers, desire altering
everything in its glowing light, as the artist
endows those yellow flowers – even cut
and stuck in a vase – with such a fire
that centuries do not suffice to put it out.
Poor Vincent, how we love his story, how it
puts the spur of gold to art; we are mad

for the moment when the story turns,
when greatness, mocked by circumstance,
turns toward the light, time sets
the record straight. Although it comes
too late, posterity arrives. Great art will out,
the Philistines (somehow) live only now.
How we adore the whole trajectory:
the gorgeous art, the squalor
of ideals, self-mutilation, suicide,
the delicious details, and then the hairpin
turns of time and taste – the lines outside
the Rijksmuseum, the million replicas,
the going price on the original, and
as the gavel falls, we take the final bid
as vindication. But of what?
What is it, then, that wins?

The incendiary flowers of Van Gogh, bought
for a borrowed fortune, repossessed, gold

flowers burning in an air-conditioned vault
in Tokyo, stored in the bank's locked
underground, next to the great fault on which
the island sits – when the Kanto quake
awakens horror in the night and rifts begin
to open in the streets and in the soul, when
the great plates grind, earth gnashes
its teeth, those glowing petals
will be ground to dust, folded under
in the new shape things will take,
the way the gods put on whatever guise
they happen on, those old tectonic gods who
move because they have to move, whose dance is
endless, and confined –

                    as in the game girls ask
if they are loved (*he loves me, he loves me not*)
so one by one, the gods
pull off their petals
and reveal themselves – the way that boys
amuse themselves with dragonflies
by pulling off their wings.

Killing the Grubs

Indra, perhaps, is the god to invoke,
or some other deity of multiplicity
I do not understand, for nothing
in the Bible, or the noble, bloody *Iliad* – roots
sunk deep in partiality and war – has anything
to say about the grubs, nor how one grab
to raise a dead plant from the ground
reveals a scurrying of capsules, animate and
gray, disgusting as things are that live
in dark, when suddenly exposed,
unmediated, to the light –
                                    I wasn't prepared
for the fury with which I grabbed the trowel
and stabbed at the wounded ground –
stabbed and stabbed, more angry as each
rubbery dot rushed off, and then I went
inside for chemicals in which I don't believe,
but there was nothing that I would not do
in order to exterminate those creeping
hidden lives.
                    For they most dreadfully
have dogged my dreams, and while I slept,
undermined the plants that shared my garden's
soil and shade. They are so obvious a sign
of what we cannot see, of what devours us,
what gnaws there now, and at
the roots – my god! I raise the trowel
again, and strike and strike. These little
scapegoats, for which I feel not one shred
of remorse, not one – I want them dead.
I am their executioner, and I exult. And yet,
they are so many, and so small, it is so
dark down there – I'll never get them all.

Middle-Class Vantage

We found this small, dry rise with a nice view,
the smell of pine, and the sound of water running by,
and here we pitched our little canvas tent,

a temporary pyramid with an open side,
its flaps pulled back. The site is insignificant,
just a pleasant prospect and a place to rest:

the salmon run is past, the trout are small and
somnolent, the breeze is slight, the next town down
the road much like the one before – the general store,

the antique shop with dreadful little cups, chipped,
pansy faces half worn off, the jewelry in a dusty case
from the sale of some estate, things lost without

their history, and maybe a Victorian house or two,
gaily painted in the palette of imaginary time, the color
of lilacs and ersatz lime, and here and there a real dog

to animate the scene. It's all a bit too green, quick water
in this drowsy channel slows, while autumn slides
its razor in the seams, the wind comes up,

the tent flaps stir, and something like a burr
sticks to the heart, and nothing can shake it off.
Situated as we are, we watch the river coursing on,

carrying whatever debris has fallen to its current ways,
and that is when we see familiar shapes go whirling by,
carried who knows where; helpless, we watch

from the banks, as we see ourselves float by –
all we can think to do is wave, wave from the water,
wave from the shore, *hello, hello; goodbye, goodbye.*

Dinner Party

The fire is lit in the hearth, and flickers.
    It is this minute exactly. Helen steps
from the shadows of the room. The room
    is stone, and the woman – all he had heard.
Paris, the aesthete, connoisseur of sculpted
    flesh, arbiter of marble,
looks at her with a gaze so intense that she,
    though aware of her effect on others, is
newly glazed in his eyes, an urn just pulled
    from the fire, with its armor of pearl. She wears
pale gray robes; her jewels are the frozen honey
    of amber that the hearth fire catches and
swirls into a molten gold. Paris turns
    the exquisite ring on his finger, toys with it,
envies her grace a little, her icy detachment,
    and turns away in a weariness it took centuries
to ripen, an idleness no occupation can touch,
    perfection itself cloys – and his eye falls
on the oiled body of the boy who is
    pouring the wine for Helen, the boy who is
watching Helen, watching her breath stir
    the hovering dust, watching and breaking
his heart over her. Now they are being called
    to the table and to whatever desultory
conversation they can devise. While she
    watches Paris, and Paris the boy, and the boy
Helen, Menelaus is thinking of his messenger,
    running toward Mycenae, perhaps, even now,
entering the Lion Gate, carrying a letter
    to his brother, Agamemnon, proposing
that they join forces in conquest, together
    take Troy, rich fortress corrupted by treasures –

a ripe fruit, half-rotted and ready to fall.

    And, his eyes lit by the flames, he turns
to his honored guest Paris, whose gaze

    he has followed, and smiling, the host
lifts his cup, and calls for more wine.

Judgment

When they removed the bandages
from Justice's eyes, she had long since
gone blind. She had been too many days
in the dark, too long alone with
the scale in her numb hands; she could
no longer tell the true from the false.
She had stood so many years in the cold
outside the courts, as the law rushed
past, clinging to the sleeve
of power – until the chill
had turned her veins to marble,
her eyes to opalescent stone.

Yet those who tore the veil away
could swear they were being watched,
and though it must have been a bit of glass
that caught a ray of sun, it was not unlike
a bright, appraising eye. Whatever it was,
they felt caught out, ashamed,
and late at night, at home, they locked
their windows tight and slipped into the room
where the children slept, and looking down
on them – for what they couldn't say – they wept.

On Ethnic Definitions

In the Jewish Cemetery in Prague,
the ghetto was so small, so little
space for the living, and less (by rights)
for the dead – the bodies were buried
standing up: the underground
train to Sheol, packed
for the rush hour of ghosts – when
the train arrives, when the final trump
sounds and the Saved dead rise,
with a sigh, they'll at last lie down.

What Was Going On

For Melanie, and her "Lilith"

There is a garden, far from our idea of it.
It is a real place, not what we dreamed,
a place where the spirits fled and hid
when wrath consumed the well-tilled fields,
when cities burned in the fire men save
for those they give themselves the right
to kill. Sodom, for instance, a nice
town; people just trying to get by on the desert's
edge. Or Hue, famed for its delicate temples,
whose trees, on that last day, seemed to bow
before they exploded in flame. The Buddha sat
unmoved in a puddle of fire, lizards
refused to let go of the wall, rice grains
clung to the bowl. Until, after a time,
in the charred litter of the sacred site,
the smoke seemed to collect itself and lifted
in a long swirl of gray, and the wind
took it to the garden, where the exiled
and the lost are found, where what had been
banished, and was presumed to be dead,
nevertheless went on, building its own
past – no less real for being invisible
to the nightblind eyes of the world.

It is night in the garden, the owl is in its element.
Here, dragging her dark silks, her hair
another veil, the wind her voice, roams
Lilith – she who escaped the ark, who
would not pair, who wept as the floods rose,
unrepentant, as she sat on the high, ruined wall
of Eden, in a crouch like a bird of prey,

who looks out now at the distant cities
like handfuls of glowing embers strewn on a plain,
and her cry is beyond our poor language:
it is a wound in the ear, the sound
of cloth tearing, of sirens,
of the terrible silence
that comes after
a crime.

Ode to Innocence

What is that sound, like a foghorn but no sea near?

The night they put the ring in the bull's nose,
he bellowed in that low-down hollow way bulls have,
through the whole long dark and into the dreams
of the sleeping children, and next day, they
woke to a difference they couldn't find, as if
something had drowned in the night.

       Years later, Madrid. The gallant
young bull enters the ring, prancing, snorting,
lively as morning, confused a little by the shouting
crowd, and yet so confident, so trusting
of the force of his own health and the humans
who have provided, always, for his need –
sweet cows must be the reward they plan, and grass
at the end of it, an endless field of green.
That's when the picadors rode in. Huge men
on horses, carrying sticks with long metal spikes,
and they stuck him, and stuck him, martyred him
like Sebastian, one thrust after another, till blood ran
from each carefully planted, each gaily decorated pick,
till it was hard to tell the ribbons tied on the picks
from the thin streams of blood pouring from each
of them, pain as decor on the flank.
And when he was tired, winded, beginning to
die, stumbling about the ring trying to escape
the pain to which he was pinned –

                           enter
the matador, all gold-embroidered show, who,
in the last round of the bull's disgrace, waves
again and again, a huge cape in his face,

until the bull, flagging but furious, makes
a last feeble charge, seeing the red wash of blood
in his own failing eyes – now the matador
plunged in the sword, and slow, like an ancient
city toppling slowly into the sea when
the earth moved under it, the bull sank
to his knees, and gave his head a last shake
of something like disbelief, and died.

If a bare hour in the pasture must suffice
for the long tunnel into the hot sun, and the crowd,
hungry, restless; if this was their pleasure –
what chance did she have, I ask you?
The ring was there waiting. The sound of doors
slamming. The echoing tread approaching
down a corridor of stone. The sound
of the crowd, its roar, and the bull,
the bull with a man's head, knowing.

Better the pond than that,
                              better to go down singing, a bunch
of flowers perfuming the air, your last sight of earth
the sun in the leaves, and the blue sky turning…

while the court did what courts do, watched and did nothing,
reported back to the throne how it all went down:
the flowers, her smile, how slowly she sank,
and the singing. For, oh, she must have been mad,
what proved it to them was the singing.

The Pillar

There are days like this, when the dry air
of the desert, with its billowing clouds
of sand and heat, less real than mirage,
the merest shimmer, suddenly
ignites the mind
where a tall column of salt
stands like a sentinel
at the edge of the Dead Sea.

And sheep come to it,
goats and their kids,
and lick and lick,
so that slowly,
from all those
tongues, it begins
to suggest a figure –
forgotten, forbidden
from the beginning,
a graven image,
a linga
standing between
sand and sky
at the edge
of a salten sea,
nibbled and licked,
tongues
shaping it
to the endless
animal need
to feed the red sea
of the interior.
It is mute and faceless,

pure shape
without speech –
and it shines, the crystals
of salt turning light
into brilliance, so that
for miles and miles
it burns like a beacon,
and legions come
and fall down before it,
bring it small gifts
and offerings, until soon
around the glittering pillar, piles
of stones and the litter of prayers grow higher
and higher, until at last nothing can be seen
except a mound of pebbles, and nearby,
a sheep bleating, salt-starved,
abandoned by the edge
of a dead sea, stunned in the hard light,
its dirty fur a blur of gray in the eye.

Now we must – one by one – remove these pebbles,
not because it was wrong to have brought them,
nor because the offering was unworthy,
nor their placement here entirely without cause –
but because it must always happen again:
one generation to bring gifts, another
to carry it all away again; one
to bury what they came to honor, another
to bring it to light again;
and always,
standing alongside, sending its small round
cries into the night, the desolate sheep
bleating for salt, its need driving us
as we bend our backs to the task.

II. *The Cohort*

Facing into It

FOR LARRY LEVIS

So it is here, then, after so long, and after all –
as the light turns in the leaves in the old golden
way of fall,
        as the small beasts dig to the place
at the roots where survival waits, cowardly crouching
in the dark,
        as the branches begin to stretch into winter,
freed of their cheerful burden of green, then

    it comes home, the flea-ridden bitch of desolation,
a thin dog with its ribs exposed like a lesson
in mathematics, in subtraction; it comes home, to find its bowl
empty – then the numberless
things for which to be grateful dissolve
like the steam from a fire just doused with water
on a day of overcast grays, lined
by a cold slanting rain –
                  it is October, that season when Death
goes public, costumed, when the talking heads
on the TV screen float up smiling at the terrible
news, their skin alight with the same strange glow
fish give off when they have been dead a week or more,
as the gas company adds odor for warning
that the lines may be leaking, the sweet smell of disaster
hanging, invisible, in the air, a moment
before you strike the match –

it is then, brother, that I think of you, of your Caravaggio,
of the head of Goliath swung by its hair,
wearing the artist's own weary expression,
exhausted of everything but its desire

for that beautiful David he used to be; and I think
of all the boys walking the streets
each carrying the severed head of the man
he will become – and the way I bear it is
to think of you, grinning, riding high in the cart leaving
the scene, a pair of huge horses hauling the wagon,
a fine mist rising from their damp shoulders,
unconcerned with what hangs, nailed
to the museum walls – luckily
the fall of Icarus has nothing to do with them,
nor the ruined Goliath who fell like a forest,
nor the wretched Salomes with their blood-splattered
platters, nor the huge stone griffins sobbing
at the gates to Valhalla as the litters are carried past…

the dark eyes of the horses are opaque with wisdom,
their hoofs strike the pavements with such a musical decision,
the derisive curl of their lips is so like the mysterious
smile on the angel at Chartres, on Kuan Yin, on the dolphin,
as they pull the cart safe through the blizzards
of Main Street, the snow slowly swallowing the signs
though the crossing light beckons –
a soft glowing green like some spectral Eden
in the blank white swirl of the storm.

The stallion neighs once, sends a warm cloud
of breath into the snow-filled air,
and the mare isn't scared yet – at least
she's still pulling. There's a barn out there
somewhere, as they plow through the light's
yellow aura of caution, its warm glow
foretelling what hides in the storm:
a stall full of gold, where the soul –
that magician – can wallow
and winter in straw.

A Poem of Exile

FOR NELL ALTIZER

The boat is always going by, set afloat
on memory's long river,
the ink that wet the wolf-tail
brush to draw the shadow on the scroll
where the eye can follow it away
from the place of origin, familiar roofs,
the worn board at the corner that marked
the turn, the name of the street illegible,
the familiar sights of home –
the trees fighting with the people
for the meager water, the little light. Home,
the place nostalgia enameled like cloisonné –
the past outlined in gold, its glaze
a shimmer of reds, perpetual green,
a shocked intensity of blue.

Here, before the boat began its aimless
journey into loss, he had been born,
bright from the first, a monarch among moths,
a restless mind that hated the relentless
seasons with their cycles and their priests, a mind
better suited for brush and abacus, the ancient figures
moving darkly in the bright cloud of the mind,
delicate footprints of thought on the paper
path – the boy was chosen out to study, sit
for the Imperial exam, was chosen
for the role of those who managed power
for an Emperor whose hem they sometimes
glimpsed as it swept through the keyhole gate.

Though freed from the yoke of laden
buckets that the village people wore, he bore
the weight of royal caprice, the enmity of peers
more ambitious, less endowed; he bore
the blame for battles lost, for peasant rage
at their conscription, taxes, empty bowls.
Hostage to the Emperor's good name,
the blame was his, and one day he was sent
like those who went before, their boats
leaves floating on the muddy waters
of the flooded streams. Exile was the end
of gifts, of privilege, decades of study,
the memorizing of a thousand years of thought.

He knew by heart the poems: wet sleeves,
loss of place, the vanity of striving and
the victory of its petty cousin, strife;
he could recite 10,000 poems of exile –
a cold moon seen (and often so)
through a broken roof; the last view
of a wife as the falling snow obscures
the dwindling pier on which she stands;
the world of dew the sun drinks back;
the poems he'd read while dreaming
of a place at court, those lines
that seemed to him abstract,
sadness that philosophy made sweet.

He dipped the brush in the dark
and forced it to a pattern on the page:
a small boat floating down a river wide
as the sky at night, jittering stars floating at its side,
and nothing visible along the shores,
the current taking it farther and farther
from anywhere – there, a bit more water in the ink,

a quick turn of the wrist – carrying its great burden
of mind along a coast where there is nothing
he can recognize, no dialect he knows,
and only the characters he makes
to comfort him – though, look, the moon
floats there beside him, heaven's lily, as he poles
alone along the looming foreign shore.

Filling in the Blanks

for Constance Merritt

Blank verse, as good as Marlowe's mighty line –
the power line on which the bird sits
trembles from the grip of its claws, from
its loving, angry song. When the bird lifts off,
the line goes on throbbing for a long time,
the message travels across a continent,
hurtles the Great Divide. The air hums here.

⌒

Word after word, the climber feels her way
along time's ledge. The wind is strong
on the face of it; what we can know
is only the feel of rock, the bite of the pilon
into the unforgiving wall, and the rope
by which we know that there are others on
the line, as we crawl across the huge blank
face – roped together by the words,
the line that is our writing on the wall.

⌒

Our game of words: hardscrabble farming
where we scratch a living from the ground,
and yours the piece most valuable to draw –
the blank, because it's undetermined, free
like some unfettered soul, can make
a meaningless array of letters
signify, and so the game goes on,
the words of one connect with the other's
words, until the board, once an empty

grid of squares, becomes a maze of sense,
like fields seen from the air...
and how shall that compare, you ask,
with the incommensurate truth?
Here: corn, alfalfa, wheat –
and there: Ruth gleaning the empty
rows, and nothing, nothing
but hunger, rage without words, and
overhead, the circling, screaming birds.

Salute to Donald Davie

Imagine David, how a single
stone sufficed him.
                  We bow
before frugality of means,
we who hunt our whales
in a troubled sea of tongues, syntax
unspooling like a harpoon rope
with a rush that leaves
the windlass smoking.
The planks of the deck
complain; the ship threatens
to tear itself apart – what with the waves,
what with its terrible, restless cargo.

What groans with magnitude,
a wilderness of ways, inheritance
of these great plains, a hopefulness
we honestly can't help – looks back
to you, to England, for lost scale:
the Norman keep, the Saxon
axial tree, the limit and the lark,
a poet who is the master of his craft,
the country church of stone,
its windows clearest glass,
its nave clerestory lit.
A prodigal returns,
though only for a visit.

Working the Block

FOR TONY

Here is the sweet punk priest who brings
the smoking entrails
to the altar, weeping helplessly for
the sacrificed pig, seeing its pink shining
face, its small suspicious eyes, its mouth
beginning to leak saliva as if it had some
foretaste, some perverse appetite
for its own extinction; I see this priest,
his fists clenched over this mess of pottage,
this last in a long trail of cut throats,
these innards which the ancestors took
for signs, reading the long turns
as if the road to the future lay down them.
I see him standing above the smoking ruins
of a life it took a million millennia to put
together, standing there, at the sharp edge
of despair, wondering what kind of deal
this was – and walking away from the altar,
leaving the signs unread. Though
in the next tent the fortuneteller goes on
reading her frayed cards, sticky with sweat
and the years of handling, her crystal
ball wearing the distorted faces
of her clients, bent on knowing the future.

Nearby, in his backyard, Death is
at the clothesline, hanging up
his black sails. When he goes out to rig
them again, we'll be working
the street, friend, stopping everyone,
passing out these flyers
that say: Save the Pig.

Her Body is Private

                            in spite of all
the sweet inducements to disrobe
in the public eye, to sunbathe
in the hot glow of the spotlight (not be
forgotten for a minute, maybe two);
                            in spite of all
the cash that flows to those
who wear their heart, not on their sleeve
in that old innocence, but on their naked
wrist, or butt, like a tattoo;
                            in spite of all
emoluments, of shrinks who swear
that secrets eat the lining from the guts
and that the more you tell, the less
you burn in hells intestinal;
                            in spite of all,
her memory, like her body, is
her own, and serpents guard it
like a tree with treasure in a myth;
if you approach, she'll turn
the blank side of her words, a shield
to the light, to fix your face
in the bright circle
of its mirror. This time Medusa
has the shield, and the last word.

On the Road to Larry Robin's Bookstore

are many monsters – the ashes of the members
of MOVE – Goode memories, the splashed blood
on the marble steps from the latest murder,
the comforting sight of safe sex – its wilted,
cast-off condoms, the needles that line the back
streets like the floors of a forest of pine, and everywhere
the warm steam of dog shit, the reeling passers-by –
eyes as blank as Orphan Annie's; the stands
where they sell umbrellas from Hong Kong
that break in the first rainstorm; the brisk
Koreans cutting endless melons into small
squares for the passing lawyers who carry them
in little plastic boxes up thirty floors
to rooms where they grind the faces of the poor
in the towers that Rouse built
and for which he has paid
no taxes; or the stale pretzels
which carbon-date to some time before
the signing of the Declaration, smeared with mustard
whose color is a yellow never seen in nature, the hot dogs
resembling that dear part removed
from her husband by America's latest celebrity;

till at last we step over
the homeless and the potholes
for which our city is justly famous,
and enter the small door
to one of the last independent bookstores
being slowly crushed to death, like the hero
of a tale by Poe, by the closing in of Borders –
we pass through its serious downstairs with
the literature of social redemption, and climb

the winding, disintegrating stair to the chamber
of horrors where the happy voyeurs lounge
among porno, magazines where the body count
is boundless, and where we, among friends and
lovers of meaning, make our last stand
for the language – in that squalor where the muse,
that battered hag, tears her split hairs,
and rattling her bones, squats and stirs
the cauldron of art, happy to be back
at Robin's, happy to feel so at home.

PHILADELPHIA, MARCH 24, 1996
100 POETS READING FOR ROBIN'S

Women Talking

FOR HILDA RAZ

There are some, do you know them?
who will talk and talk and talk (I am one)
until the trees drop their leaves with exhaustion
the fish in the river hide under rocks
and the sun covers its face for shame
under the moving clouds whose glow
is all we can really see, ever,
of what we mean –
                   who nevertheless go on
talking, spinning sentences out into air
like a demented spider, a Whitman in
drag, a sage or a Sagan obscuring
the cosmos with his huge
talking head...

Still, there are times when
the great stone wheels that grind wheat
falter; times when the wind abates
and the grass moves as slightly as the fur
of the cat when the child, sleeping, breathes
on its silk; times when the man who walks
through the streets of the cities, ringing
his brass bell and reading
the edicts of kings, mumbles,
falls silent, his lantern gutters out –
                   then the mother tongue flickers
like a warm fire over the world, and the world
quickens, and a woman of fewer words (this is
you) – each word vibrant
with the hidden life of its own silence
and the clear beauty of its absolute

attachment to what it agrees
to relinquish, syllable
by syllable, into the endless variation
of the sky – sends up
the talkers, the explainers, the panters after
meaning (this is me) – like smoke from
the burning field, the prairie that
depends on its own burning, whose roots
are a tangled web under the soil, waiting
for the wind to catch
what the lightning
ignited – all the overgrown
thicket. In its place, a green furze
of beginning, a cricket,
a nerve ticking
at the neck, the wrist,
those signs –
all that is
needful.

"...now I can go on and on"

– Elizabeth Bishop, quoted in a poem
by Nell Altizer

like snow, white repetitions of the cold,
no two the same (said Gertrude Stein) and yet
to all intents and purposes, they do repeat:
white white   white white   white white
they make a sheet...oh shit – the barometer
falls more; already the degrees have dropped
like climbers falling from a ledge, left zero
far behind, and plummet endlessly through
night; no light, between these sheets of ice,
above, below – all the indications
are of snow. More snow.

The sky is gray, and reminiscent of the void.
The gray is uniform, confederate, sad hue
of the losing side, the color bled away; it seems
that warmth in any form must be a dream
stoked in the fireplaces of the mind, the halcyon
hearth of make-believe where a log ignites
and blue flames lick along the bark,
and throw their heat; the flames cavort
on the wired grid of the brain, its firescreen:
bright winter tales to warm the neighborhood,
fictions which confound the winter's loss,
accounts of old kings shriven, Perdita found,
queens restored from icy marble
to a pinkish froth of breathing health...
to hell with what is frozen in the beaks
of crows, those worms like popsicles;
to hell with Minnesota, drop the ice
in Scotch and soda – to hell with snow!

And hello, Nell. Take heart,
the calendar's prophetic: spring will come,
though it bring stress (for April is the cruelest
month) – Hallmark cards are on the side of light,
and who are we, mere trolls of language
at the bridge of thought, to speak, however well,
of endless nought? Well, who indeed?
And, in all this snow, why not?

"...*Zero at the Bone*"

FOR MARIANNE BORUCH

I've never seen a field on fire, a field
of moss, I mean – that slow burrowing of fire
under the prairie's skin, that slow burn
that goes on for months and years...but I have
smelled the peat smoke that blights the Irish air
and warms a thousand hearths; and I have seen
a forest fire turn the whole sky ochre
for a hundred miles, while just below
the forest floor, the fire wakes the sleeping seeds;
and I have seen the hundred tongues
of Kilauea, molten streams of glowing red
sliding like reluctant serpents from below
the crust of cooling lava tubes, to pour
into the foaming ocean in a wrath of steam,
as from its fiery heart, Earth extends its reach:
these living fires I've seen –

but not those gods of calcium and lime,
the mineral gods of time who slowly burn
that cosmic fuse to which the universe is tied,
creators who choose fossils as their form,
rattle dried planets like a gambler with his dice,
or geodes with their crystals of stopped star
that grow so imperceptibly that only eyes
of glass can track their path into a final ice;
gods with cold silver smoldering in their veins,
the slow burn of the universe
that numbs the mind with the relentless
numbers of the Second Law –
the gods with x-ray eyes, who love to watch
the clacking bones inside the living flesh

until the world is but a dance of death
like a medieval mural on a wall –

                                        well, pal,
as the world goes on, slowly dying of its life,
we will be sitting at the table by the stream,
gnawing at the bones; we'll suck the marrow
with its rich red fix of iron and of salt,
undaunted by the way the sun keeps
setting in the steel vault of heaven,
the way the packets will arrive
no matter what. But never
fear, though the moss
somewhere is
burning,
it isn't
here.
Not
yet.

III. *Lifelines*

You, Failed Pronoun

Direct address to the swans: you, whose feet
are now unbuttoned from the snow, your wings
spread wide and white, heading out of here,
back to the breeding ponds of spring, away
from freezing lakes whose sudden ice closed in,
when you had thought yourself south enough, and safe;
you had to be cut loose by the Wildlife Service,
and so make your escape, entirely out
of vision's range – gone even your ghosts at Coole.

Once you have flown, the slate is blank,
the great mimetic circle cleared of imagery,
dark as the inside of a camera when the lens
is closed. Now what shall we do for a *you*? Now
that the winged ones are gone, the moon drowned
in the pond, shattered by a tossed stone, the wheel
a drone in the darkened air – to whom should the voice
address itself, and who should the speaker be?
For who, anyway, are we?

Silence. Arrows of asparagus stand fastened
to the ground. Green fence against thought,
image from the armory. Everywhere: thickets,
thorn bush, briar patch, hedge – screen that
dims the light; grids of complex, senseless
green. Dense, ambiguous web. Mind's wallow.
In it, a chartreuse flash, slim bright thread
on a dark ground. Eft. Splash. Gone.

Job's Wife, A Twentieth-Century Casting Script

> Thy sons and daughters were eating and drinking wine in their
> eldest brother's house; and, behold, there came a great wind from
> across the wilderness, and smote the four corners of the house,
> and it fell upon the young people, and they are dead...
> JOB, 1:18–20

Job's wife, bereft, without
appeal, when God made his devilish bet
that torture would not break the faith
of Job – a story to rightfully upset
the bearded men who sat around
the glowing fire of their Book, arguing
the days away, endlessly debating
what it meant, day into night they shook
their fingers at one another, until, exhausted
at last, they prayed together, slept,
began again at dawn – quoting scripture,
quoting Rabbi this and Rebbe that, hardly
noticing the food that now and then appeared
or the scolding women who brought it,
or that, outside, their enemies drew near, or
that a wind was bringing ruin, or the horror
that lived always in the hills was once more
grumbling in its den, about to descend again.
A test! they'd say, after, counting the dead,
a test from a doubtful God, unsure of us.

How tired she must have been
of his pieties, this mad attempt
to plot the runic script of chance, or
to retail value out of wholesale death,
the slaughter of the innocents – dead children
whose skin was parchment
on which the future faded like an ink

dried in the sun, blank scripture of noon.
Sandpapered by dust and grief,
she swept the tents, in silence, swept.
Though the text puts words in her mouth,
a bitter question and a curse: "Dost
thou still hold fast thine integrity?
Curse God, and die."

But what did they know of her –
how pity swept her like a storm
when she would sit, pulling a stick slowly
through the dust, watching the wind
erase her mark, the cursive line
that longing makes when it drags itself
along the ground, searching like a serpent for an egg
or something round to enter and be fed, oh then,
she would feel such sorrow for them all
forced to view horror
and make a story of it,
these depressed savants, who,
their own death coming like a funnel
of whirling sand across the wide expanse
of dunes, as the horizon disappeared,
set up a wall of argument,
fell into a perfect panic of faith. For
even the best of them could protect
no one, least of all himself.

Then let us assume she went in
to join the old man, he who had
had it all – flocks, robes of office, gold,
and most of all, a cause for these effects.
And she sat down with him in the dust,
watching the red sun begin to drench the far
hills, and they spoke to one another at last,
and it was not of God they spoke.

Off the Hook

Rain on the dock, cold, in a place
for which there is no map, only a slack
line between you and the dark waters, a line
that sways and disappears in the oily surge,
no hint of where it might lead, so that
when the line all at once goes taut,
so tight you can feel the long nerve in the arm
like a hot wire, the muscle pure tension
around it – you are forced to pay out
some line, and let whatever moves in the dark
begin to explore the limits of freedom,
to know the full weight and resistance
of what is pitted against it, so that you,
hauling it in, have become its deadline, unwitting
at first, and soon after, unwilling, as you feel
the wrenched muscle that is pulling out there
as a tearing in here...
                         that's when
the line goes slack again.
You reel in a loose scrawl of line,
like a child's scribble on the wet page
of water, and pull it into the air – the end
is broken off clean, like the thread
you bite off in your teeth
when the stitched seam is finished.
The water is quiet. And your mouth
aches from having clenched
your teeth so hard, and somewhere,
deep within, a knot of scar tissue
must be sealing the place
where something had bled,
as if from the bend of a hook.

Conditional Riff

If we could find a way to turn the wind toward home
If there were more than one to hold the rope
If there were only three to turn the wheel
If there were ten who sang in darkness, wearing shawls
If there were, over all, the arc of sky
If it were bright and marked with stars
If we could see from that how small
If we could learn from that where then
If we could ever be that near
If we could, without insisting, call
If we could move in unison but not in ranks
If we could care less for the walls
If we could find the niche without the wall
If it were able to be hid
If it were able to be found
If it were anything at all that could be said
    we might have said it and been free
    we might have followed it and seen
    we might have seen it open to the rain
    we might forget the constant of complaint
    we might have known
        the flower's trumpet throat
        the sweetness deep within
        the silver thread that's drawn
        the honey one drop at a time
        the drop of syrup on the tongue
    how easy it would be

Winged Victory

The spokes of light and shadow, the golden scale,
    balance, symmetry, the *contraposto* of the stone,
the way the marble folds of drapery mimic
    the pressure of the wind when a body fronts it,
Victory perched on the prow, her great raptor wings
    spread wide, like banners flying, sails unfurled –
Nike, Victory. Except the image has no head, no arms; it is
    a torso with a gorgeous body in a vibrant shroud
and winged, the crown of the winding museum stair,
    the camera's darling, the headless fair, the victory
of dismemberment, its triumph even over stone.

Somewhere, in history's rubble, lies Victory's head –
    in Sarajevo's ruined precincts, or in among
the fallen pillars of Olympia, or deep below the Dead
    Sea's brine, or on the Great Plains where
the bones of the buffalo glint in the sun; it stares up
    with vacant eyes at the vast and turning sky,
and is more silent than rising smoke. It is no
    Orpheus, it does not sing. Its mouth is a rictus. It grins.
A thin wolf, out hunting for her cubs, all milk and fur and
    earnest need, slinks past it in the cliff's scree,
where it is one more stone among stones.

The Aztec capital, by prophecy, was built on the rock
    where an eagle sat with talons clamped on a snake,
drilling its beak into the writhing flesh. There
    a city rose on an island in the Lake of the Moon
whose waters fed the great metropolis, made waterways
    and mirrored the bridges, causeways, palaces,
the sun, the flight of eagles in the sky. The great city lies
    there still – Tenochtitlán – it shimmers in the broken mirror

of memory, mirage of light and tears, Cortés,
     still standing at Montezuma's side, gazing from
the temple heights at the resplendent city spread below. He wrote

to his king in Spain: "*we saw the bridges on the three cause-*
     ways…through which the water of the lake flowed
in and out…and we beheld on that great lake a great multitude
     of canoes…and we saw in those cities…oratories
like towers and fortresses and all gleaming white, and it was
     a wonderful thing to behold." After the guests' surprise
attack, and their retreat, the smallpox spread in Tenochtitlán.
     Besieged, the waterways cut off, the city became an open grave.
Cortés returned, burned parks and aviaries full of birds, sank
     the floating gardens, pulled down whatever stood. "*I intended*
to attack and slay them all," Cortés wrote. "*The people of the city*

had to walk upon their dead while others swam or drowned in the waters
     of that wide lake…indeed, so great was their suffering
that it was beyond our understanding how they could endure it."
     Quetzalcoatl covers his face with his wings. The altars
fester in the heat of noon, the god drags his coils, his bloody
     plumes, along the ruined walls, slides down the steep stairs
of the Pyramid of the Sun, his trail a dark illegible script that ends
     with a flick of the tail as it vanishes into earth. The eagle's
nest is empty; the snake it killed has eaten its eggs. At the feet
     of Cortés lies Victory's head, a vulture picks at
its eyes – marble, inedible, blind from the start.

࿆

At the Sapporo Snow Festival
     on the northern island of Japan, the army,
bound by the ashes of the past to the martial
     arts of peace, has turned its many arms
to building sculptures out of snow and ice.

In one wide field of white on the outskirts
of the town, the soldiers man mock fortresses
of snow, each one with an icy chute
for the children to slide down. They climb inside,
then reappear at the top of the slide, bright
snowsuits a blur of color as they fly down
into the waiting arms. The soldiers catch them,
set them, smiling, back on their feet on the hard-packed
snow. Nearby, a folktale, told in figures carved
in ice, catches the brilliant winter sun: a rabbit
makes his way across the backs of sharks
who have formed a bridge to save him from
the ocean waves: a figure waits on the island
he is about to reach, translucent arms outstretched
like rays, her head a blaze of light.

Amaterasu Omikami, someone says; she is the August,
Sacred Sun, melting slowly in her life-bestowing light.

Of a Sun She Can Remember

After they had been in the woods,
after the living tongue woke Helen's
hand, afterwards they went back
to the little house of exile, Annie and
Helen, who had lived in the silent
dark, like a bat without radar in
the back of a cave, and she picked up
the broken doll she had dismembered
that morning in her rage, and limb
by limb, her agile fingers moving
with their fine intelligence over each
part, she re-membered the little figure
of the human, and, though she
was inside now, and it was still dark,
she remembered the missing sun
with a slow wash of warmth
on her shoulders, on her back –
as when you step shivering out of
a dank shade into the sun's sudden
balm – and as the warmth spread,
it felt like the other side of water,
and that is when she knew how
light on water looks, and she put
her outspread hands into the idea
of it, and she lifted the lines of light,
crosshatched like a web, out of
the water, and, dripping, stretched
the golden net of meaning in the light.

Blessing

this is not the truth
about the end   but a hint about
beginning   When the Buddha
had sat alone
for nearly forever
beneath the tree of many names
when he had taken into himself
all the suffering there is
and will always be   then
he did not despair
he turned away
from the empty air
that starving saints exhale
he laughed   at the idea
of nothing   What he saw
clear and unmistakable
before him and really on all sides
was a lake   and the lake shone
and there was light in it
and he knew   that to hold
all that water in his gaze
would mislead him
about his own
size   unless he entered the water
and bathed
for there is no enlightenment
without immersion

And so   after so long   the Buddha
entered enlightenment
which is not the end
but the end of being alone

and the Buddha   whom the world
had thought sufficient
unto himself   was not
for that was what
enlightenment taught

And at the end of
so long alone
the Buddha slowly turned
toward all the others
who were also alone
and she opened her arms
and around them all   the water
stretched   and shone

The Messenger

The messenger runs, not carrying the news
  of victory, or defeat; the messenger, unresting,
    has always been running, the wind before and behind him,
      across the turning back of earth, leaving
        his tracks across the plains, his ropes
          hanging from the ledges of mountains;
              for centuries, millennia, he has been running
                carrying whatever it is that cannot be
              put down: it is rolled in a tube
            made of hide, carefully, to keep it dry
          as he runs, through storms and monsoons,
sometimes on foot, sometimes poling a boat
  through a flooded mangrove swamp, or
    setting stiff sails to cross from island to island
      running before the wind. In some ages, peasants
        have helped him – bringing him small cakes
          of rice wrapped in the weeds of the sea and
            new sandals woven of hemp for his torn
            bleeding feet; sometimes in the heat of noon
          they would offer a drink of rosewater, sometimes
        a coat of fur against the winter snows;
and sometimes at night, he would rest
  by a fire where voices wove with the music
    of gut-strings, or with mountain pipes whose
      sound was like wind through the bones
        of creation – and he would be cheered
          by the company of others, the firelit glow
            of their faces like a bright raft afloat in the dark;
          at times, rumors spread of his death, scholars
        analyzed his obsession, dated his bones, his prayer bundle;
      but at dawn, he always arose, in the mists,
    in the blur of so many mornings, so many shoes

worn into scraps and discarded, so many
  the cities that burned as he passed
    them, so many the skulls abandoned
      by armies, so many whose blood
        stained the threads of their prayer rugs,
          so many, so many, so many –
      oh,
    and that green, sunlit hill that kept
  rising from the dark waters of flood, outlined bright
against the sky, the odds, the evidence –
and he, the messenger,
running through history, carries this small tube,
  its durable hide – carries it, not like
    a torch, no, nothing so blazing;
      not like the brass lamp that summons
        a genie, no magic wishes;
        not like the candles that hope sets aflame
      and a breath can extinguish…

no.
  He carried it like
    what has no likeness,
      what is curled up inside and
        he swore he could feel it, though
          perhaps he had dreamed it, still
            at times, stopping under some tree
          or other, when the night was warm,
        so close the stars seemed to breathe in
      the branches, he would lie quiet,
    then it would seem
  that whatever it was in there
    would pulse softly with light, a code
      only the heart could break
        (but of course he couldn't say
          for he was only the messenger) –

and at sunrise, wearily, he would rise
  to his feet and trudge on, sometimes
    running, sometimes stumbling,
      carrying whatever it was that could not
        be put down, would not be cast aside –
      and besides, he would chide himself,
    weren't they all as tired as he,
  and hadn't they helped him, time
and again, on his way?

Up Against It

The wall was white, whitewash lime
that shines in the sun till white is pure pain
searing the eyes.
                       And the wall was marked,
pocked by a spray of black holes, like nothing
so much as the dots in a child's puzzle, waiting
for a line to make sense of them, to pull
from a scatter of points, a familiar shape.

At the beginning of the bad time
we have come to think of as usual, they stood
a man here, against this wall, simply because
of what he was, something that made it hard
to do what they wanted,
                              so they thought that
if they killed him first, at the very beginning,
the rest would come easy, his blood like a red
door opening into the future in which the gypsy
wind, capricious, always eluding them,
would be stilled, tied in a sack;
and the everyday which wore them
down into grit under its heels, would disappear
into clouds of power; their boots would be real
leather, the rawhide smell from what they had taken
and hadn't the time to cure.

And if he were Lorca, García Lorca, the writer
with a fire in his hands (and he was) –
and if they stood him up against this wall
in its white that defeated the light, throwing it back
like a knife into the eyes – and if, in that moment,
as they raised their guns, he remembered

a dream he had dreamed but a month
before, a dream of a lamb surrounded and butchered
by shepherds –

if all this were true (and it is) – then
we approach this wall at our cost, counting its black
holes like the shrunken emblems of the cosmos eating
back its own matter – and what then?

Shall we paste up the placards
of a revolution in which we no longer believe? Shall we
tear down the wall, knowing another stands behind it,
and another, and another, to the horizon of counting?
Shall we line up the children beside it,
pointing at each hole as a lesson
through which, like a sieve,
their hope will begin
to drain out?

Or shall we plant flowering vines along the wall
to cover the record?
And when each tendril, each slow,
wavering filament,
each unruly, winding line of green
is swaying along the wall,
looking for somewhere to anchor
its urge to go on growing
(*verde, te quiero verde*),
what then?

Why, by then, in the long twilights, in the hard work
of planting and watering, of watching and waiting,
by then we may have understood what we can't now
imagine, desperate as we are about the white wall, the holes
in the shape of a man, the mark they wanted to leave us,

the line terror taught us to trace –

so different

from the one that he left, the one whose

shape left its trace in the heart, the balcony open,

the long spill of stars in the sky, the track

of creation's milky tongue, and, listen –

the shift and seethe of the sap

forcing its slow way toward the branching

twigs – the ear-splitting crack

as the end is riven by budding –

a salt breeze in the orchard,

the small leaves trembling with light.

FROM *Otherwise* (1993)

I.

Night Fishing in the Sound

The sound is dark; you can barely hear
the gauze-wrapped warning song
of bells, and cannot see
the buoys swinging on top
the oily waves, the water a black
so absolute it drinks light
back, unquenchable thirst
like that the shades in Hades had
for the hot blood of sacrifice –
how the dead swell, like ticks,
till they rise, bloated envoys
out of the envious dark.

The waves of the sound sway
endlessly, a restless channel caught
between two seas – one fresh, the other salt –
as if suspended between hope and
certain sorrow. And you, in a small craft,
having left behind the little inland
sea, are tossed in all this roiling dark;
the trick is to play the wind
for time, sinking the line
deep into the heaving black, trying
not to stare at the dizzying lantern swinging
over the deck, a drunken sun on a pendulum;
trying to keep your equilibrium
with no horizon to steady the eye, riding
the dark sound blind, hoping for fish,
wanting to reel in, to reach the end
of the passage, but afraid

of the waiting ocean, the enormous dawn
when light, rising from below, seems to come
from everywhere at once, tsunami of
overwhelming sun.

But still there is
the solid feel of the helm
under your hand, worn grain
of wood that fits the grasp
and steers the little craft
out of the rocking cradle of the dark,
safe, into the cauldron of dawn.

Being As I Was, How Could I Help...

It was the noise that drew me first,
even before the scent. The long water
had brought something to my den, spilling
its banks, leaving the hollow pod
of reeds in the cool mud. Whatever it was,
it cried inside, and an odor rose
from it – man-smell but sweeter.
Two small hairless cubs were in it, pink
as summer oleander, waving
the little worm-like things they had
instead of paws. Naked like that, they
made my blood go slow, my dugs
begin to drip. I tipped the pod, they slid
into the ferns, I nuzzled the howling
pair, they found my side, they suckled
there and drank their fill. That night
the red star in the sky was bright,
a vulture's eye that waits
with a patience that I hardly understand.
The twin cubs slept in their shining
skin, warm at my side. I dreamed:

The trees were falling, one by one,
the sound deafening, the dust that rose
from one, a mist to hide the felling
of the next. The mountains were
cut in two; great stones were rolled
and piled like hills until the sky
was shut; where the trees
had grown, pillars of stone rose
high, the birds circled, but
their skulls struck the sky.

Teeth chewed the earth; our den fell in
like a rotted log when weight is
added to decay; nothing to eat, the cubs
howled, the flesh fell from our bones,
we ran under a strange sky whose light
was wrong: it rose from the city walls,
bounced off the leaden heaven – flat
as the sound of a stone striking mud.
One of the brothers killed the other.
Blood poured where the streams had run.

Nowhere to drink, we slink from one rock
to the next, hunger drives us to the walls
where, sharp as the eyes of men, death
waits with its thousand iron thorns.

But the warm sun woke me. I forgot.
The twins were all I saw, for days
we lay together by the den, the river
ran beside us like a friend; they drank
and laughed at the morning light
that played in the shelter
of the leaves. Forgive me,
I was wolf, and could not help
the love that flowed from me to them,
the thin sweet river of milk.
Even now, though the world has come
to match the dream, I think
I would give it again.

When Asked to Lie Down on the Altar

FOR MARIE HOWE, AND HER "ISAAC"

A guiding hand raised
above us, haloed in sun, the glint
of silver on the blade like the sheen
of sperm...
                  there was the boy,
tadpole swimming upriver, a miracle
about to unravel again, the birth
a matter (each time) of amazement,
and there, on the hill, as always,
sharpening his knife, the sad man
with the headache, the servants,
the high opinion of himself, the sand
it was built on, the mountain
his stand-in – raising its stones
toward the heavens, straining against the rain,
the wind, the merciless years that were wearing it
down, inexorably, the undulant way
that stone is worn
by the tongue of the rivers...
                      so, lowering himself
on the woman – the pride of his flocks, the power
of his tents in his member – he launches
this Isaac, tail still thrashing, who
grows in that inland sea where
the children of deserts lie down in still
waters, and there, in the placid place
of beginning, rock in the haven of dark.

Back on that mountain, the cold
dry air of an unforgiving
climate, the father

forces the animal on to the stone,
and now, the sun draws nearer,
the sweat pours into our eyes
and blurs our sight, so we can no longer
tell which is the boy Isaac, which is
the ram, for when the man
looks down he sees, in the face
of the boy looking up at him, the wet
eyes of the uncomprehending sheep, and
as he buries his fingers in the ram's
deep wool, he feels the bony shoulders
of his son, and everywhere (is it
the heat?) the world swims in red, and
his hands, the stones, the altar, the split
side of the mountain, the curve of the earth
run with it, the rivers are stained
with it, the tides are a strange burnt
umber, the waves wash into the shores
the color of rusted iron, the red
of a knife that has lost its edge,
that has spent years exposed
to the rain, so when you reach
to pick it up, it crumbles in your hand
like a cake of dried mud, and the air
picks up the grains of it, moving
them in slow spirals of dust
and smoke, sending them
like signals toward
a lost tribe
in a buried village
of tents folded like the wings
of dead moths
under the burned-out lamp
of heaven.

And it wasn't a lamb, but the strong ram
of manhood we dreamed, women
dipping our urns again, and again
into the darkening well;

                    it was not a son
but the man himself we lost, the man
who sacrificed what might have been
to his fear, and who came home
a stranger to the tent
smelling of blood
and the death
of what we had stayed for,
late, after the others
had given up hope,
after the others
had changed
to receive him.

"...as soft and as pink as a nursery..."

This is the good child
in his bed. Beside him, his mother
with her sweet pink face, her nice
manners, her extremely well-manicured
fingers, her strange desire to have him
perfectly untouched, so that her hands
are always running over him,
pushing his hair back and exposing
his hot, gleaming face, wiping
his nose with the edge
of her tissue, picking
at things on his clothes: little bits
of thread, dust, food, lint
of a world that clings to him
almost lovingly – these she assiduously removes
as if she were his valet
grooming him for a starring role, the curtain
about to go up, and only her between him
and the humiliating abyss
of some unforgivable gaffe,
the laughter of strangers...

this is the good mother
who, as the light fades to mauve
and the corners begin to fill with distended
shadows, reads him stories full of vengeful,
hairy, bad-tempered and evil-smelling
monsters, huge as Hindenburgs, engorged
with centuries of crimes imagined
in millions of nurseries, waxing
in the growing dark of bedtime; genies
festering with long imprisonment – planning

at first, gold and deep gratitude
to their rescuers; later, after years
in the jar, beginning to plot
the gifts that bring ruin; finally,
bloated with a rage
so murderous, so purely tabloid
and horribly true, that to lift out the cork
were to loose Pandora's swarm of evils
without a hope to flutter after...

the little boy can do nothing but watch
as these colossal figures fill the little space
that is his room, their thick legs rising
like the trunks of redwoods, their distant
shoulders looming like cliffs, their necks
periscopes peering into the black intangible
sky, from where he hears, booming,
the arrogrant thunder of their laughter
so that even the stars are shaken
as if the night were a thick black mass
of icy gelatin in which the stars
were caught, shivering and burning...

he draws himself up tight under the quilt,
a still, small mound that watches
round-eyed as the monsters pour
from the pink heart-shaped mouth
of his mother, who now and then smiles sweetly,
calls him her little man, her bug, her pet,
and fiddles with the button at her neck.

The Love of What is Not

1. Cityscape

The eye is trapped in a cul-de-sac –
the street's a half-lit box, the sky a lid.
Now and then you can hear the pop pop pop
of semi-automatics down the block. Dawn,
the waste is everywhere – the gutters run
with it, the trash turns to a black gum
in the rain and builds a silt of sewage
along the curbs. Every pile of bundled rags
breathes with a labored heave, the anonymous
rise and fall of drugged lungs; every steam vent
wears a human cover, the underground
exhales its saving heat.
                         It feels late
in the Middle Ages, and sure enough,
there on the corner are those made mad
by God, blocking the way, branding
with their damning words the young
who pass with lowered heads
heading for the women's clinic door.
You can almost smell the burning flesh
as the words make contact, sear.
"Murderers!" one shouts, wild with need,
conviction. But of what? What moves
the zealots who rise at dawn
to arm themselves with signs –
against what foe?
What is the furnace of this heat?

        One carries, on a stick,
the crescent image, enormously enlarged,

of some creature from an underwater realm –
huge head, unformed arms, its marbled
eyes sightless, its shape not human yet,
exposed, and magnified by loss:
is this a last-ditch loyalty
to what she might have been? –
the bud that never opened to the sun,
the unlived life she carries
like a fetus suspended inside
a bottle of formaldehyde
in a medical museum.

This is the city we have made:
blank walls of brick, shining
towers of steel and glass, gutters
running with waste, the living
dead, and there, its sign –
a tender embryonic thing
exposed, as if the city wore
its unborn soul outside itself,
torn out and held up
to the light, huge fetus
in a hydrogen balloon,
its string cut, floating
now, above the City Hall,
into the blue, growing
smaller and smaller, shrinking
until it is no larger than
an atom of dust,
the prick
of a pin,
this
period .

II. E.T., I-U, AND THAT OLD-TIME RELIGION

Up there, on the movie screen
a strange encounter happens: the old celestial
dream, its jasper stone and gates of pearl,
lowers from the sky; with bated breath
the faithful watch this miracle occur,
and wait, eyes huge with hope.
"*I John saw the holy city, new Jerusalem, coming down
from God out of heaven*... BEHOLD, I MAKE ALL THINGS
NEW." And so it descends, singing, a gospel
UFO, resplendent with the jeweled lights
of Revelation, yet landing like a hovercraft,
and opening its shining steel side, it
lowers a gangplank to disgorge
our saviors from the sky,
as the script implies they are to be.

But what emerges from this sci-fi craft
sent from the blue dominion of a naive faith
is a crew to break the heart – huge
fetal heads and ancient eyes, raw skin
so thin it shows the pulsing veins, and limbs
so new and delicate they are barely
flesh at all, tender lives so fresh and
vulnerable you want to stow them back
inside imagination's womb until they're ready
for the sudden light. Nothing
really happens after that. The film ends.
The red exit lights beckon.
No one can imagine what comes next.

Unless E.T., a brother to this otherworldly,
fetal crew, suggests how it must always end
when neoplasm, forming

deep within – made visible by biotech,
a ruby privacy undone – is put to the service
of that death-defying belief
that we are not
of this world, that some unseen high command
will lower through the air one day, like
a helicopter to a battlefield, and save us.

E. T. departs, riding an old idea,
diminishing out there, alien, far from the child
who spawned him, rocketed out into the cold
lightless expanse of outer space. We watch,
the helpless audience of a great commercial
success, as our innermost chance, the fresh
being of our planetary soul, its return
to itself, to the earth out of which it comes,
hurtles out and out and out, alien,
alone, towards a nowhere
we were always told
was home.

Amelia

We had lived centuries apart. The imperial
soul had its gardens, far from home, where
fancy held its court, fiction made its peace,
lost horizons, sunless caverns, miles
from where the gleaming pearls of spit
lay in the unpaved streets – those seething seas
of mud or tunnels of dust; twin buckets
across the shoulders on a yoke, the slosh
of night soil going to the fields
to coax the rice through the steaming paddies'
mirrors, to fill a hunger we could not
have dreamed. The jangle of coins that buys
only the smell of meat. On the market table's block
the pig's head leers, its eyes like marbles
lost in a haze of flies; nearby the baskets
of dried scorpions, medicinal skins of snake –
a lifetime shed, a landing strip is
suddenly klieg-lit: Madame Chiang
Kai-shek smiling in the newsreel film,
stepping delicately down the silver stairs
of a shining plane to America, her arms
laden with roses; her body chic
and slim in a sheath of Chinese silk,
her English as smooth, impeccable.

What did we know
of the river near Chongqing
filling with bodies like a human soup;
what did we know of the people
marching north, burning with ideals,
brilliant Mao with his almost female face,
his growing force a pincers to pull

the rotten tooth of Chiang Kai-shek
from China's aching mouth. What
did we know – nice American kids
wearing the tinted glasses that
Dorothy wore to dim the glare
of Oz, green fire from a lake
of burning ice. How we yearned to be Madame
Chiang Kai-shek, cool, clicking her mahjongg
tiles, enchanted, a distant song, elusive
as the other who flew through the pages of LIFE –
brave Amelia, remember? the woman who fell
from the skies. Amelia Earhart, lost in flight,
all the lost years ago.
                        Through one we ruled,
by proxy, but through Amelia we lived,
around some distant river's
idle bend, in dense forests
where no sign of mangled craft
was ever found. So few paths to choose –
we chose those two: the one who flew away
and fell from sight; the other
one – the General's wife.

The General's wife has long since been
disgraced, the silk veil torn, the fist
with its painted nails pried apart.
But Amelia lives on, as real
to us as Arthur was
to the English tribe who dreamed
of his return. Our distant hope
careens across the skies – spy
satellite that spins and scans
the lush Pacific isles – until below,
what is that gleam? Adjust the focus
of the close-up lens, and watch

(among the layered masks of green
the island wears) the image grow
and clear: shed carapace
of steel and cast-off wings; nearby,
a woman moving by the tangled bank
along the stream. And being still
American, we see her in a beam
of light, alone, in all the secrecy
of public glare, the dream itself
a bit theatrical.
                    She stops to gaze
into the pool where stones have
steadied the water for self-portraiture:
she sees her hair, grown long and white,
a shimmering face that smiles
through a network of lines. "Lost
for good," she thinks, and smiles back,
then takes a step aside. The second
her image is gone, she sees
the scene grown suddenly wide, a world
of green, profuse and noisy with life:
the hum of hives and villages,
the flowers with their open, lurid lives,
the insect drone, the chatter of monkeys, constant cry of birds,
and in the water's pause – an overflowing bowl
of sky and scudding clouds.

Admonition

You are
their sister. Nevertheless
they accuse you of the worst.
When you defend yourself
they call you
defensive. Beware –
you who traffic with
the wet nurses
of history, those iron nipples,
that acid drink,
pure and deadly.

Operations: Desert Shield, Desert Storm

1.

Who
are these two women, walking
through the great forum of the plain, walking
under the sun's blinded white eye,
under a hard, featureless sky, bright steel
without a trace of blue. Two women,
their shadows trailing them
like assassins.

What
are they speaking of,
so rapt in conversation they scarcely
seem to see the vacancy through which
they walk. One kicks reflexively at bits
of junk that litter the dry ground, raising
white spurts of dust that hover
at their feet like slavish hounds
of cloud, assiduous on the trail of
all lost things.
                    It is as if time itself
were a dry fountain, where the urn fills only
with pale ashes; where broken tablets
of illegible laws cobble the ground;
where church and court alike are built of bones,
a filigreed white lattice-work of chalk
through which the white sun casts
a black lace of shadows, widows' weeds;
where a small wind picks through debris,
an indigent in search of scraps; where,
in the desert of our god-drenched origins

the armies grow again, human beetles in
their masks, vague hatred with its poison
gas, the air itself a deadly trench
to these benighted boys, condemned
to fall again into the ranks
of what repeats: into the breach
once more, another city broken open like
a rotting fruit, the flies rising,
the delicate seeds exposed
to the sun, a book with a broken
spine, anything where enough
is left to name.

Antigone and Ismene,
or so we might call them,
these two women walking across this page
of history, this page that is not
a page, because no one can turn it, because
it extends and extends, the smoking cities
scattered like open lesions
to the periphery of sight, these wounds
that memory worries so they
cannot close, this sand
littered with the bodies of brothers.
These two women, whoever they might be,
have the look of those daughters
caught in the line of a self-blinded king
(a father who is also a brother)
debating again the choice
of terms – imprisoned in life, or death.
One is full of argument and heat,
an intellect who can face down a tyrant
with her tongue. The other has a downcast
face and sorrow even in the way her garments
hang, folds that hold the shadows deep

inside; though young, her soul
weighs like an ancient thing; Ismene
takes her sister's arm, to whom her life
is bound, for whose futility she feels
such a ravaged pity, and such
affection she agrees to lose
their argument, pretend to a weakness
she could never own, because she knows
the anger of Antigone must speak
although it end as an echo in a chamber
sealed in the granite hills, a tomb
whose stone is always rolled away
too late. Ismene, grieving,
lives, and walks the olive groves
alone, a lively shade for company.

Again, the dictator
in his empty boots
stalks the narrowing tunnels
of the streets, his little voice
widened by the megaphones of war,
death's echo amplified.
And then it is Ismene
recalls her sister to her side,
steels herself to animate
that shade, and lose her yet again,
if lose she must.

II.

What vicious agency of farce
recalled that ancient sister's act
of love, that wish for a brother's
burial? The stage darkens, the shadows
of the sisters merge, and deepen
to a common night:
                    the end of light
those young men, living, saw
(to think that horror stops the mind)
as the earthmovers pushed the tons of sand
up over them, and then rolled on.

And after the cheering crowds have gone
home, after the last yellow ribbon of sun
has faded in the west, where shall Ismene hide
when they open the cave where defiance
hangs, when those swaying sandals
brush her face, after they cut
the body down, where shall she turn
from all that is buried in the desert plot
made for headlines and parades,
a place too dry for even grief.
Yesterday's news.
Too topical for poems.
Welcome home, this is
America, welcome home.

Bat Cave

The cave looked much like any other
from a little distance but
as we approached, came almost
to its mouth, we saw its walls within
that slanted up into a dome
were beating like a wild black lung –
it was plastered and hung with
the pulsing bodies of bats, the organ
music of the body's deep
interior, alive, the sacred cave
with its ten thousand gleaming eyes
near the clustered rocks
where the sea beat with the leather
wings of its own dark waves.

Below the bat-hung, throbbing walls,
an altar stood, glittering with guano,
a stucco sculpture like a Gaudi
church, berserk
Baroque, stone translated into
flux – murk and mud and the floral
extravagance of wet sand dripped
from a giant hand, giving back
blessing, excrement – return
for the first fruits offered to the gods.

We stayed outside, superior
with fear, like tourists
peering through a door, whose hanging
beads rattle in the air from
one who disappeared into the dim

interior; we thought of the caves
of Marabar, of a writer who entered
and never quite emerged –
the caves' echoing black
emptiness a tunnel in the English
soul where he is wandering still. So
the bat cave on the Bali coast, not far
from Denpasar, holds us off, and beckons…

Standing there now, at the mouth
of the cave – this time we enter, feel
inside the flutter of those
many hearts, the radiant heat of pumping
veins, the stretch of wing on bone
like a benediction, and the familiar
faces of this many-headed god,
benevolent as night is
to the weary – the way at dark
the cave releases them all,
how they must lift like the foam
on a wave breaking, how many
they are as they enter
the starlit air, and scatter
in wild wide arcs
in search of fruit, the sweet bites
of mosquito…

while the great domes of our
own kind slide open, the eye
that watches, tracks the skies,
and the huge doors roll slowly back
on the hangars, the planes
push out their noses of steel,
their wings a bright alloy

of aluminum and death, they roar
down the runways, tear into
the night, their heavy bodies fueled
from sucking at the hidden
veins of earth; they leave a trail of fire
behind them as they scar
the air, filling the dreams
of children, sleeping – anywhere,
Chicago, Baghdad – with blood,
as the bombs drop, as the world
splits open, as the mothers
reach for their own
in the night of the falling
sky, madness in
method, nature gone
into reverse...

here, nearly unperturbed,
the bats from the sacred cave
fill the night with their calls,
high-pitched, tuned to the solid world
as eyes to the spectrum of light, gnats
to the glow of a lamp – the bats
circle, the clouds wheel,
the earth turns
pulling the dome of stars
among the spinning trees, blurring
the sweet globes of fruit, shaped
exactly to desire – dizzy, we swing
back to the cave on our stiff dark
wings, the sweet juice of papaya
drying on our jaws, home
to the cave, to attach ourselves
back to the pulsing dome, until,

hanging there, sated and sleepy,
we can see what was once our world
upside down as it is
and wonder whose altars
those are, white,
encrusted with shit.

UME: *Plum*

The fruit is small, and often served
shriveled, soaked in some attar or
other, an odd shade of red, weak and
toward the blue. Sometimes one
of these unpromising tiny plums
is set in the center
of a flat bed of white rice, to mime
the nation's flag – red sun
on a white field. Those years ago, we never
knew, kept ignorant of all that might
disable war, that the flag with the wide
red rays, that rose over the bodies,
adorned the Zero's wings, was a war flag,
emblem of a burning sun, like rage
or whatever it is that sets men's lives
at nought, and pours them, young
and hot, down history's drain.

The trees here must be bred for the beauty
of their flower, for the plums are sour, the cherries
small and bitter – but, oh, the *ume* blooming
in the early spring, the *sakura* unfolding
in a brilliant sky, blossoms borrowing
the light for shelter – a glowing parasol
of pink and white, or
the world a child's globe
that sits in the Buddha's hand
and when he laughs, it shakes, until
the air is filled with silken snow,
the wind toying with it, lifting
the petals as if back to the branch,
then bringing them lightly down.

Walking the shimmering tunnel of flowering
trees along the Imperial moat, Mrs. Nakano
and I spoke of the war, when we were
both children (the same age, I think,
though it was a point of pride with her
to never say). Her voice was
matter-of-fact, or else it was
the way English goes flat in a mouth
made for another tongue.
In Kobe, she had crouched with her
mother in the bomb shelter while our
planes bombed her city flat. The trees
shivered a little, the delicate arbor
sent down a shower of petals
to our feet. The carp, grown huge, slid by
in the moat, and the rain began, steady;
we opened our umbrellas
as we went. She spoke then
about her husband, her misery
with him, his anger and his mother,
the doors that one by one
she'd tried and found them locked.

How do we keep from going mad? I thought, looking
at the trees bred for their beauty
by an aesthetic breed of men, who
wanted a woman wrapped in tissue-thin silk,
her mouth a hole with blackened teeth,
who would dive at the dark stack of a ship
to a fiery death. And saw, with them, our own
young men, the same, filing into the black
belly of a huge cargo plane, each with a woman
in his wallet, her words on lilac paper,
her distant image as his aphrodisiac
in hell. I tried to ask the question that can't

be asked in words – having no subject and no predicate
but death. I thought of the bombs falling, and
then my mind went blank as the radar screen
when the thing that moves into its range
is much too close, or gone.

And Mrs. Nakano and I, the fortunate ones,
walked side by side beneath the cherry trees
and watched the great smoking craters
of memory fill in and disappear, and watched
the rain turn the fallen petals
into a sticky debris, and walked
because we were alive, and walked
to keep from going mad, and walked
for beauty, and for company,
the whole perimeter of the Emperor's moat,
that carp-infested fence around
the palace, walled in,
where power keeps its face,
and ends, as history ends, in Lear –
old, heartsore – the dead
Cordelia in his arms. Reverse Pietà,
a motherless world, the father
holding the sacrificed child
on a ground of fallen petals
wet with rain, plum
on a field of white.

But here, we break the circle, cross
the street, and bow.
We part, Mrs. Nakano
and I, go, each
to her own
gate.

II.

The Bird in the Laurel's Song

How long have I been here? I can't recall
how many suns have risen and withdrawn
since I came down to this branch to rest.

How strange it felt at first, warm
under my feet, and when I landed here
and clamped my claws around its bark
I could have sworn I heard a moan. Is this
the work of men, I wondered then,
who like to decoy us with images of wood
we take for friend, then lay in wait for us, armed,
their arrows tipped with our own feathers.
Yet this was opposite of that – a tree that feels
like wood, an ordinary laurel, leaves a polished
green, but with a pulse inside, I swear,
the engine of a heart like mine; and something
not quite planted in its stance – the way it swayed
and seemed to reach out toward me as I passed.
And so I stopped, and sat.
                              But I'm uneasy
now, the forest ways are broken here,
some sadness haunts this tree
that I fear, mortally, to sound. Nor can I sing
when these leaves rustle in the air
around my perch, and breathe and whisper
in my ear, and speak of what I cannot
bear, nor compass with my airborne
mind – some deep attachment to the ground
whose price is to be rooted there; it makes
my wings ache with the thought, and
I must fly away from here – but yet am held
in dappled light like a net of lace

that will not let me go. O gods,
if you can break the spell that holds us
both together in this glade, then I will
stay with what it is within that suffers here.

> The laurel stirred in a passing wind, and the sun,
> aslant on the river's back, moved
> in a shiver of gold, and a woman appeared
> by the river's bank, looked around
> as if awakened from a dream, a little dazed.
> She reached down to pick the book up
> that had fallen at her side, and following
> the water's edge, she wandered off,
> singing to herself.

But it was I who sang,
though I look out through her eyes;
it is I whom the gods hear, I who laid down
my wings, and nested here out of love.

How to Get in the Best Magazines

Preferred:
tired little poems, taut,
world-weary, properly bored
with it all, though still a bit awed
by atrocity, choosy
among the data, the minutiae
in which we live – hikers
caught in a biting swarm of black flies.
Look for the few words, the image
to catch, exactly, ennui; the odd bone
of a finger sticking through the sod
of the freshly laid lawn, something
small, dry and horrible
to prod us, to stick in the craw
for a moment – a brief sign
of remembrance
between the ads for Neiman Marcus
and the Inn with exclusive arrangements,
its own private bay and a dock.

Produce, please, a poem that will fit
in a slot between fiction and furs, one
to go down like a silky martini,
chilled from its small bout with the ice,
leaving only the green globe of olive,
tiny and gone in a bite, its acid tang
lingering around the pit, small
and hard in your mouth –
the one bit of grit
is what's wanted, that pearl
beyond price: there
is the minimal poem, the absolute

disappointment, the one
you will want
to submit.

If, sadly, you slipped, inserted a bird,
loud on the sill in its lush spray of feathers,
or a scurry of feet in a bed of heartsease,
a green as layered and dense as a Balinese
screen, a light air, angelic tread
of sunlight on the water, a climate
of friends, an afternoon's sufficiency
among so many summers –
rejection must follow,
as surely as suburbs
in the wake of the cities.

If we, who have cost the world so much
additional suffering, who are so heedless
in plunder,
                    if we could not, this afternoon
or some other, be happy, replete,
or harvest at least
some richness out of the native
air;
        if we can only perfect
the thin arts of unhappiness,
the tongue's anorexia
playing its riff in the hollow
horn of plenty, the world a mere
annex to the mortgaged house
of our discontent,
                            then

it is time to write
the acceptable poem –
ice and glass, with its splinter
of bone, its pit
of an olive,
the dregs
of the cup of abundance,
useless spill of gold
from the thresher, the dust
of it filling the sunlight, the chum
broadcast on the black waters
and the fish
    – the beautiful, ravenous fish –
refusing to rise.

The Muse

There she was, for centuries, the big
broad with the luscious tits, the secret
smile, a toga of translucent silk, cool
hand on the shoulder of the suffering
poet – the tease who made him
squeeze those great words out. He
was the mirror *and* the lamp, she the torch
who burned with the blue butane of a pure
refusal, too good for mortal use, her breath
was cold as mountain streams, the chill
of the eternal – no hint of plaque
or any odor of decay. Ethereal as hell,
a spirit in chiffon, the mystery is
how she had got so rounded in the butt
and all her better parts as soft as butter,
why such a wraith should be so ample,
what her endowments had to do
with that for which she set example –
all this was surely Mystery, oh that elusive
object of desire, that 'untouch'd bride
of quietness,' that plump poetic dish
who lived on air but looked
as if she dined on pasta.

Basta!
A pox on the great Lacan
who writes with his eraser, on all poetic
Graces, mute and pensive, concave exactly
where he is most extensive – oh look
what she has *not* that he has got,
a thing I'm too polite to mention
except to say it rhymes with Venus,

it was the Latin word for tail;
its root, therefore, is not the same as pen
which comes from the word for feather.

But enough of these fine distinctions.
What a great tradition was born when
Alexander whipped his penknife out, cut
the knot she carefully had tied, leaped
on his mount, a perfect straddle
and let the crotch decide
who was the horse and who was the rider,
who was the muse and who
the writer.

Leda's Handmaiden

I was Leda's intimate, and slave,
born, as I was, on the losing side,
where the mind grows agile,
and the heart's true tongue
learns to put on fable for disguise.
Take, for example, the swan –
it came to me as we shook
the pillows out and a few white feathers
flew. How she laughed when I spoke
the thought aloud – how we'd say the god
had raped her in the swan's white shape
with the winged ease of miracle,
but big, believable: the serpent's neck,
the malign eye, the yellow webs
of its feet pinning her arms,
the terrible beak – Zeus,
a perfect cover for a king too old for love
in whom the dry seed rattled like a gourd.
Now I look back, I think perhaps
the fabrication a mistake – fuel to set
the bright sparks of desire ablaze,
a whetstone to ambition's
extra axe-bright edge.

Though everything can be forgotten
(or so sunk in memory's swamp
that the shape to which emotion clings
is lost), consequence goes on,
the unexpected spawn of our exploits,
and even of our lies – like Leda's pair
of girls, the pawns of fame,
her joy of them left out like babies

for the pigs to eat. Her boys, gold stars
hung in a mother's pane. Murder and war,
and the animal roar of a city
put to the torch – born from those nights
of love. I think of his tread
on the porch, the dust of his boots
on her floor, the thick Persian lamb
of his hair. How afterwards
Leda and I gave rumor wings, shaking
swan's-down on her bed, airing out
the sweet male smell of sperm,
for the seed of gods is
odorless, like light.

It was I who led him to her room
and I who told the story
that the lyre takes
from court to court, and I, who had him
first, and after, too, for he was
mine – the sons he got of me, oh...
two were drowned at sea, two died
at the walls of Troy, one lives
to prune the olive trees, but
is not whole. Our daughters,
practiced in the arts of grief, are
widows all. Cold beds, moth-eaten coats
hung on history's hook, a name
that flutters like a sleeve.
And the children left behind –
for them I fill the vacancy
with tales, to guide the plow
that furrows memory, the gift
of a lady's slave, poured
into the ear of a war-blinded son
who is a comfort to my age,

that one – because he loves
the tales I tell, because
he sings them in a cadence
that would crack a stone
god's heart; at night
when sleep despises me,
I write them down,
I sign the name
we share.

Ambition

I didn't always think Penelope
a fool. We used to play together
when we were girls, and she could
outswim anyone, and on a dare would
grab a dolphin's fin and ride the wind
across the island's bay, or shinny up
a tree and swing from the highest branch
as if the gods had not invented
fear. I was more cautious by far,
more prone to seeing things
before wind blew the smoke away – I'd see
the bones before the fire was out,
the blood before the blow was struck,
the storm when it was still a mile
out. But that is like me, isn't
it, to bring the tale around, back
to myself? It is Penelope I meant
to tell you more about, and how she
changed when she met him, the wily
one, Odysseus, my callow brother.
For I am Nobody's sister, the name
he took to trick the bullies, before
he could afford his own. His fame
is now on every tongue, well known
to the widows of Ithaca, a curse
in the mouths of the women
he ordered hung – his concubines
who lay with other men the twenty
years when he was gone. Lord
of Ithaca, bowlegged, strutting
about the town, telling everyone
tales, Mr. Adventurer, the brilliant

leader who came home alone –
his ships sunk, his men
bones for the sea to rattle.

Penelope was wildest of us all,
her mind as agile as an ibex
on a mountain wall, skipping
from one outrageous notion to
the next, never slipping or losing
her footing. Quick to anger, she was
always sorry after. A fire
seemed to flicker over her; it caught
when her first blood came. A woman's
first blood is her bright signature
of life; a man's first blood is wound –
his own, another's, blood shed
in war, or torn from a girl
he forces, or the deer he pins
with arrows to the earth. So her desire
for him brought fear into her heart, as Kore
picks each spring those flowers
whose roots, when pulled, will rouse up
Hell. She who would be ruled by nobody
became his fool.
                    My brother. As a boy
he had been sent to study war and numbers
somewhere far across the sea, the place
where sun arises, gold and yawning, from his couch
each dawn. And bright as a god returning
he must have seemed to her, for she,
my wild friend, gazed at him – something
in her blazed, then seemed to freeze. She turned
the way the goat's milk turns
to cheese – she seemed
to thicken and grow solid; she left

her bright self in the sun
of memory, wanting
nothing but to hover in his shade.

And how he loved it, for a while –
he must have slept with everyone
he saw once he had tired
of having her. And when her belly
swelled with Telemachus, he was off
to war, his son grew up without him,
while she became his living monument,
his name carved in the deep grooves
of her brain. The endless shroud she wove
was never finished; she didn't have to
struggle anymore – he was her great
excuse: frame, thread and pattern:
liar brother, tale spinner.
                       Our other brother
I loved well, and truly – he was my friend,
whose name was folded in the flames
that took him. We poured so many treasures
on it, such libations, his pyre lit the skies
for days. Had he lived to be the one
to rule the island, perhaps it
might have gone another way.
And how I wished Penelope
had chosen wisely. But this is
how it goes – she chose mirage, the sheen
of distance, a shield's flash, wave-foam struck by sun.
So now our island's poor, our women bitter, the children rootless,
there is this tiresome couple – old Odysseus
bragging of his exploits, stony Penelope
dragging through the halls, and me,
Nobody's sister, who
all the time was

plotting
another story
in which our better brother
lives, in which Penelope
keeps her wild wits
about her, I finally get the part
I wanted – it is my
fingers on the lyre, Apollo's
whore, I who tore the hearts
of Ithaca, as cloth is torn
for tourniquets
to staunch the pouring blood;
my song that called the moon
to wrap the sea back sweet around
the island, to make the marble pebbles chuckle
on the beach each time a wave receded;
my song that made them
love the orchards of abundant olive,
the laden vines of peace, and
made them
hate the dogs of glory
and laugh
with the gods' own laughter
catching Ares
in bed with Aphrodite –
stupid beauty, dazed and
drunken war.

The Lament of the Valkyrie

Always the fair extensions of his will,
we'd had no thought but him – his chill
our misty climate, the air we breathed;
a gloomy god, full of dark forebodings, empty
of regrets. At his feet, a pair of silver wolves;
ravens for epaulettes, and war for sport.

I forget the day it began to sicken me,
notwithstanding the sweet rewards
of such a role, its bright celebrity;
and not just me, the others too,
began to hate this lottery –
the choosing of the slain.

When did the armor's weight seem more than flesh
could bear – the silver sheen we'd polished
to a rival shine with moon, so when we rode,
the battlefield's red flares played over our steel skins
in jagged tints of fire, the Aurora Borealis
of the northern skies – the glorious shimmer of war?

Was it the day when, swooping in, collecting heroes
for the gods to set like bloody dolls
along the trestle tables in Valhalla's deathless
halls – our horses suddenly reared, refused
to answer to the rein, their nostrils
wide, indignant, at the smell?

Was it then we first looked down and saw
that blighted spring, as if awakened from a mead-
soaked dream, what rain uncovered at our feet,
half-mired in mud – mere boys, eighteen
or less, oozing the blood, the brains, the seed
meant to quicken life again?

And saw, as if our eyes were newly made,
how the mud matted their hair to the same dull slate
as their eyes, cold embers on which the breath
of myth could blow, to kingdom come
or Götterdämmerung, and never
bring the least glow back to those dead eyes.

So we dismounted, led our anxious horses
from the field, put down our shields, and knelt
to lift the helmets from our heads, to shed
the iron weight; the clamor of our falling armor
was like the wreck of anthems; we felt
blood stir, flow back to our stiff limbs.

Our swords we kept, withdrew into the room
whose darkened corner held the loom
where we had learned the trick of weaving
murder into art; and there, in all that dusk,
we cut "the crimson web of war"
and then, our own bright plaited hair

that once had flown among the banners
luring innocence to war – outdoors
at the field's edge, shorn as winter's
lambs, we left insignias of braided gold
already beginning to darken and sink
in the merciful mud of spring.

And since it happened as I've said
(though memory too grows dark and blurs
until I can't be sure which field it was, or year) –
from ruined Valhalla's walls, why do I hear
wolves howl, the beat of raven wings,
the same old trumpet call?

The Secret Garden

The way you see it first is through
the keyhole, that aperture with hips,
and one you have to crouch down low
in front of, and squint to get a look
inside. A green space glows, oh it is
pretty, as aqueous as an aquarium,
where slender shapes, finned and neon-
spotted, glide beside your eyes, and press
their tiny noses to your glasses. Lean
closer, the keyhole holds the Mystery, until
of course, a key's inserted and spoils
the view. Meanwhile, the green invites you:
rosehips, clinging vines, the shy nasturtium,
grapes by the pound, diminutive white lilies
of the valley, pussy willows; in the shade,
moss, moss on every stone, moss crawling
the walls, moss over roots, soft, smothering
moss – underneath it all: a million worms,
brown, segmented, one end like the other,
a poem that ends the way it opens.

When it rains in the secret garden,
the worms come out and sport; they push
their wet way through the parting
particles of soil, they slip through mulch
and lift their small snub noses, faces
empty of expression as a toe, and lo,
they dance among the fallen petals, cavort
in the brackish puddles, splash and writhe
until the garden is alive with coils
and coils of shining brown (a python
if you think of them together) – until

the earth itself is pure Medusa, lost
head of blue spinning through the vacant
cosmos, its crust a fume of writhing
serpents…and that, dear Jack,
is what is in the secret garden:
you are invited to come in for tea. But
bring your own cup and a folding chair,
and do wear rubbers, as there is danger
of infection, and we should hate
to think the worms could get you
before we're through with tea.

Those Who Come After

will never say of us:
what wonderful myths they had.
There will never rise, dripping, from our midst
figures whose wings open, dry in the sun,
completed by being
more us than ourselves; what we leave
is all that can be
dredged up from wrecked harbors –
history's debris. So
in the end, it is not the beautiful figures
draped in the white silk togas of dream
nor the muscular thoughts stalking the peaks
in the golden proportions of Greece
with the lightning clenched in their fists,
nor the animal-gods with the eyes of hawks
and the delicate fingers of girls,
no – only what broke in our hands
when our voyages – like the stick in the paw
of the monkey, extending the grasp –
ended in the slow grip
of possession, as a continent's shore is
slowly swallowed by sea, making an infinite
coastline, the in and out of an edge
endlessly nibbled and gnawed. That
is the line we leave behind us,
the infinity of rat-tooth,
the posterity of loss…

But when they say of us
what we have done, perhaps, they will speak
kindly of those who, near the century's
end, pried open the hand;

of the way the wind lifted the lovely
gray spirals of ash, until our hands
were empty as a cloudless sky,
empty as altars whose offerings
had been acceptable; perhaps they will
say that there were those
who took down the harps
hung in the sorrowing trees, having lost
the taste for conquest or revenge,
and made a song
that rose in the air
as smoke rises –
at first a line, and then,
slow eddies, the spirals
endless, unwinding
the sky's blue
spool.

III.

Generic Vision, 1991

A huge figure drags a body, riddled
      with wounds, across a landscape.
                          The figure
is many stories tall, a colossus,
but migrant; its westward path is a meridian
that spans the globe. The body it drags behind
it, miles long, bumps along the ground, snags
at times on outcroppings of rock, has to be
edged over, lifted off; sometimes it disappears
in water when the figure crosses rivers,
then shears the muddy banks as it is raised,
leaving a slash where nothing grows; smears
      the earth as it is dragged along, its trail
            bright as the red tail of a kite
                  wavering across a darkening sky, a track
                      endless as the wound that feeds it,
                          an inexhaustible supply, thick black
                    fluid from a hidden source, staining
            the terrain it passes over; crushing
        towns and villages, flattening forests,
      rocks becoming gravel in its wake –
its pressure is immense,
it gouges the soft earth into
canyons, pulls the hills
down to the level of the sea.
                        The figure
who drags the body is faceless, ponderous
as stone, though its mobility argues for
the flesh, and from it something rises
like a moan, a cry
muffled by the absence
of a mouth. The bleeding load

it drags is shrouded, wrapped in
multicolored cloths and rags resembling
faded flags, torn and streaked
by constant passage.
                    The figure
moves against the turning motion
        of the Earth, its speed exactly timed
                to the planet's revolution, so that the sun
                        stays fixed above it in perpetual
                                noon; the figure casts no shadow, walking
                its treadmill way, the black blood
        gleaming in the light that goes on
searing as the days slide into years,
        the years to centuries, and the millennium,
                winding down, spirals slowly through
                        the chute of time, the empty channel
                                        we have made of it, like a worm
                        that leaves the hollow of its tunnels
                as the scripture of its path. Just so,
        the figure walks, the planet
                slowly spins the other way, the body
                        marks the road in blood; the figure
                                walks, the planet turns, the sun,
                                        through the broken ozone, burns.

What Was Left Over

for Sujata Bhatt

I.

As you said, Sujata, it was not
mentioned, was kept out
of the story, out of the elaborate ritual
of parting and redemption, the gorgeous
sanction of sacrifice – that plunge
into the heart of fire, the drugged victim
or the fear-crazed hero, the scattered
entrails of power, of belief –
but there, you described it, how the elephants
gather, how they circle, and see it; how they
see it and mourn: the torn carcass
with the head taken for the trophy room
of the gods; the stumps where a tusk
or a forest once grew;
                              the priest wiping clean
the blood of a lean season from the ritual
knife; furtive, in haste, he strips off
the splashed ceremonial garments;
                              the charwoman who scrubs
off the stone of the altar; the man who rakes up
the widow's ashes, handfuls of bone
in the embers of wood;
                              those who dispose
of the dreadful torso when the decree
to dismember has been carried out
and the crowd dispersed; who come in with a hose
to rinse the charnel-house floor;
                              those who sweep up
what is left of the monk

who clothed himself in the fiery robes
of protest at the command-post gates;
                          those who glean
after the harvest, permitted to gather
what remains, who leave the killing fields
with a small box and a stone
in the throat, a silence
that nothing will ever dislodge;
                          those who are
heart-scalded, digging the mass graves,
tipping the barrows into the trenches;
                          those who clean the tiles
of the mosque after the bomb
took the man at his prayers, who lie down
but find peace gone from their sleep;
                          all those who come after
the drama is over, all those who
have seen.

2.

Sujata, perhaps you are thinking of them
as you stand at the bathroom sink
that has replaced the communal fountain;
perhaps you are thinking of them
as you fill your cupped hands with water,
running cold from the metal faucet
in this Northern town – and now, no,
I don't know what you think, wouldn't
presume, but I know how it feels
as the cool water bathes your burning eyes,
as the same water floods mine,
from the headwaters of that river
no traveler has found –
the waters that are falling forever
down the cliff on whose edge
we find ourselves, staring together
into the endless gray, and feeling
on our skin, in our eyes, the fine
atomized silk of its spray.

Atget's Gardens

As I am now seventy years of age and without heirs or progeny
of any kind, I am extremely anxious about this collection of plates.
EUGÈNE ATGET IN A LETTER, NOV. 12, 1920

Was it always a dream   then?

the fallen leaves   the stairs
that lead nowhere   the players
flown   plates in a drawer
was anyone *ever* there?

nothing lives here but the light

it inhabits the place   hovers in
the groves of trees   inviting the eye
away from what it sees   as if
just behind the stairs   water
lapped a wall   and at the landing
stage   a boat were being untied
about to push away on the dark
water   just beyond your gaze
its opaque shadows thick
as the impasto of a dream
you can't remember
when you wake –

these bloodless scenes   all
color drained   even
memory has withdrawn

leaving only this one odd man

dragging his camera from one
beautiful emptiness to another
one space within the next
like Chinese boxes   they vanish
down the funnel of the camera's
lens, and then into the eye
of the man   who always waits
for what he can't recall   and wonders
what it was he lost

perhaps no one

ever entered here   the light
suffusing everything may only
seem departure's glow
unless it is the light
the dying sometimes see
when   like Atget they face
away   though the quiet is huge
we barely hear
the water lap and lap against
the pier   the chuckle of loose
stones   the dry rustle of
the half-lit leaves
the hush of a prow
cleaving
water

Moonsnails

The size, you said, of silver dollars
but then, the weight is wrong, for these
aren't solid things at all – the snail
mere water, the silver case a streak
of moon, of light that curls
where little perturbations of the tidal
pools send water in its spiral
tracks on which the moonlight writes,
the no man's land between
the wild tides and the stiff resistance
of the human world...here
the mudsnails snooze and dream,
while the moonsnails lie
like cast-off trails of glory
on the black mysterious backs
of secret pools, where, when the sea
has pulled away, gone so far out
the pools forget the daily
maelstroms of the tides
that, as they slide in, open
a million mouths of shell
hinged to the water's flow – when all this
hunger seems a dream, the mouths
all shut, the clams burrowed back in the silt,
not a frond stirring – then the moon
comes down to lie
on the black satin skin
of the pool, in love with life
in its shallow bed – for a moment,
a perfect round, so absolute, so
fragile that the merest breath
exhaled on the sky's dark mirror

will set the silver
wavering – illusion's
perfect circle
shuddering, is gone, and
and, in its place, moonsnails,
the shining, silver spirals
of the breath unshelled,
   turning in and out until
     the tidal flats are moiré silks,
   wind makes the ghostly moonsnails
swim and shimmer in the pools
    on night's reflected shore,
out there, stars swim in the wide black
      pool of space, mere shallows to
              the space beyond
the black night spinning out of itself
       trails of light that disappear
   into that distance
where no horizon is, where
    the universe is going out, everywhere
at once   moonsnails glimmer, spiral galaxies that spin
       on the trackless waters where the veils
        of the primordial fire hang
          at the red edge
           of sight

God, for a silver dollar in the hand,
cool heft of metal from the earth's
sweet veins, or a real moonsnail,
a tiny dish of light, but solid,
dreamless, curled inside –
its artless slice of life.

Freed from Another Context

FOR FRANCINE

1.

Here, the foreground of the other
side, and she is watching
raptors float across the blue
ground of the sky – hawk, eagle,
osprey, owl; seized from afar,
she holds the vision in the field glass
of a far-seeing eye, focused, extended,
as only the practiced eye can be,
years spent looking out, scanning
the horizon for a speck, staring at a bleak
expanse of sea, learning to interpret
every dot – a flash of fish, a falling
boy, a ship. Or if the house is set
on plains, on the cold griddle
where the glacier had its way,
the watch is lonelier still,
the hope longer, attenuated as
the freight trains stretched across
the darkened land, one line of light
to interrupt night's solid blank.
She watches with the raptor's eye,
trained on distance as she is,
and dark – so when she turns
to what is close, so intimate
and huge, she keeps the gift
of sight beyond herself,
neither sentimental nor detached.

II.

Look – a patch of snow, afloat,
the owl!

Below, soul's
shadow on the lawn, a warmth
that will not leave the hand.

III.

There is resemblance, and its sense:
the silver alive at the back
of the mirror; the fishing bird
who must find its catch
through the cast of its own shadow.

Everything moves another
thing, and that in another
way – the leaves on the oak
stir the air like oars, the fish
on the weather vane turns the wind
way around to the south, and the flight
of the owl rouses the moon
whose face on the water
awakens her, and the floor
of the world is desire's sky –
familiar feathers brush her
cheek, wings flicker
in her blood,

and the head of the owl
swivels all the way round
till the moon's dark side
swims up from the pond,
and she sees from
the other side.

The Mulch

FOR SUJATA AND MICHAEL AND JENNY MIRA

Leaning on the gold
of autumn is how it starts,
first the light in the ginkgo's
yellow leaves, then the breeze
that sets them moving
like the gold in the hold
of a Spanish galleon as it falls
slowly through the waves,
spilling its hammered bits of coin
that turn as they fall with a riffle
of light, almost a school of plated
fish, flickering through the half-
light of the undersea, before it
gets so deep, so close to winter,
that all the leaves have fallen,
the gold settled to the bottom
in the silt, turned by the rains
and the icy sleet, the layers
of damp of day after day, into
a gray amorphous mass
in which those bulbous creatures
move, segmented, smooth,
like the insides of some higher
beast, the part earth hides away
inside, or under leaves, recoils
around these slugs, the blind, unthinking
ropes on which the soil depends.
As golden leaf turns slowly into mulch,
spring tugs the stem, it rises
from the pond's deep mud; its dark green
pads, like leather wings on some prehistoric

bird still tied to water, spread out
around it, and the great bud
lifts like a pair of praying
hands, begins to open in a slow pink
spray of silk – each blossom
large as a human head, and swaying,
securely fastened on its stem;
in its center, outlandish dancing
cone, its apex down
like a spinning top
and still
inside
its seeds will start it all
again – from where they feed
on fallen gold, on fall,
when turning leaves
ripe with light
sift down around
the lotus
whose blossom rises
from deep within the mind
where, out of all we thought
forgotten,
love
prepared the flower.

Kazuko's Vision

In the blizzard's heart,
a little girl lies stretched out
on the snow, watching the sky repeat
itself in white, each flake a petal
from a cherry tree, Heaven's *Sakura*,
the great tree larger than the compass
of the eye, the snowflakes blur, obscure
the bridge that Hiroshige veiled with bits
of white, the same snow falls tonight: for time –
our little minutes, hours, histories,
small as the holes a pin makes
in a *shoji* screen – has broken
loose, and floating on the breeze's
back, drifts in the swing
of cool black air, night's loosened
hair whose sheen is like the sea
on a night when the moon is full, its
glitter scattered on black waves…
just so, the snow, as it spills from space,
floats easily, the way birds
ride the wind, look down and see
one small figure in a red
snowsuit, floating in a field
of white, and looking
up, laughing as the snowflakes fill
her eyes, her mind, the sky – until it's all
one thing: sky, self and snow, a host
of almost-same, untied, afloat
together in a dance of wind
and breath – so, one by one
by one, things fade
into each other and the snow

makes night a weightless space
where centuries
lightly pass, vanishing
like snowflakes
falling
on a lake.

American Painting, with Rain

The gates have closed to the rotted park,
amusements rusted in the rain,
the roller-coaster curve turns out
toward sea, and there the rails are
broken off, the structure hangs
in air, like wires
from a ruptured wall.

The hour grows late, the dark comes down;
the animals are wading to the ark. The day
is sinking as the waters rise; you hear
the plash of deer, of buffalo, of wolf,
who walk together, heads down,
in the thick downpour, their hides wet,
the heavy smell rising like steam,
leaving the place deserted,
a promontory view
of gray and swelling sea.

For years the English painters
composed their seascapes looking in
toward land, the ocean in the foreground,
the horizon home, the island anchoring the eye.
But here, from America, the artist,
looking out, makes the foreground land,
the horizon is the waiting sea,
its inescapable heave,
the distance crying like a hidden
baby in the night, calling out,
a promise of tomorrow, or...
The gulls circle and
scream. Something is torn.

Standing here, at the edge of the canvas,
the brush fallen, the waves crawling
over the edge of the frame, eating
away at even the notion of art,
the gray frame houses on the coast
giving way to mold and the storms
of too many winters, and the view
out there with too many waves, the sea
an infinite set of perspectives, no end
in sight, distance pouring back at us
from everywhere we look,
until vision itself is a sieve
letting the waters in, even here
in this room, safe
under the artifical lights, sure
of the concrete floor under our feet,
we feel the slow lapping of water
at our ankles, its wet crawl
toward our calves, the rising chill
as we slog toward the exit, as we move,
with the animals, wading out,
as fast as we dare through the growing
dark, and the rain, the unknown
terrain, the obstructions we can only guess
as we collide with them, their shapes disguised
in sheets of water, collecting shadows,
the uncertain lights.

As an actor fades
behind a scrim when the lights
dim – figures, walking slowly into
curtains of rain, seem oddly
not to walk away at all, but simply to
dissolve into the dot matrix
of the mist. This is not the ending we

would have chosen, trained, as we were,
in the old way, the clear outline,
the bold stroke, the lucid use
of perspective, hard light,
strong shadows.
the single
vanishing
point.

     ∽

In Hawai'i the rain comes down hard,
friendly, the forest is used to it,
the flowers in their profusion
a perennial thirst. A woman stands
in the open doorway of her house,
dreaming of Maine, of thunder and
the leaves of the maple turning
to face familiar weather. But the child
has never known anything but
the rains of Hawai'i, its trees
laden with blossoms, the stars
in the night sky so much like
the small white sweet flowers
in the dark green hedge by the door
that the heavens too must be
perfumed to the very edge
of infinitude – he doesn't yet
think these things but he is filled
with them, all the same. He stands,
leaning toward the falling water,
holding his mother's leg
for support, this little
Noah, untroubled
by the freight his name carries,

small steward of the future,
loving these rains, seeing
only the shining veils
of his bridal with
the world, standing
on the rim of the Pacific
on his island that is all of earth
to him, boundless, secure,
standing on the threshold of
the house of Sarah and Matthew,
greeting the rain.

Changing the Imperatives

And having remembered it, then –
what next? Oh, go ahead, they said, lift
the stone of memory from the heart
like the stone from the mouth
of the tomb. And are they to blame
for what stumbles out, rags
crawling with maggots and lice, into
the blinding day?

Listen, my friend, they gave you
the key to the wrong door,
the one marked Sins of the Fathers –
the one that opens onto the abyss
where obsession hangs its ladder
over the lip, where the dead
climb daily back up out of the gulf
dragging their broken bones, each day
more ruined than the one before,
until, nearly spent,
they are little more than handfuls
of powder, aroused like genies
by the slightest wind, resentful dust
that keeps the air
unbreathable.

The past. The wretched luck that,
nailed to the mast, becomes the goad
for which the ship is lost.
Take up the fallen hammer
and turning it around, pry
the nail from Ahab's gold doubloon,
then toss it over the side.

Watch how fast the ocean can forget,
how brief an opening your entry
makes, how soon the wave
shuts back upon itself, how small
a curiosity the turning bit of gold
excites as it drifts down
through the endless sift of green…
years later when the salvage men
dredge up the sand, they'll find
only a disc of gold, round
as the old threshing floors
of Crete, but small enough
to fit into the hand; the face
it wore – unrecognizable.
Then drill a hole and wear it
on a ribbon as a talisman,
relic of the gentle, veiled power –
forgetfulness, the goddess
whose name nobody knows,
whose shrines are forgotten,
her temples overgrown,
her images lost.

FROM *Sarah's Choice*
(1989)

I.

Coda, Overture

She stepped out of the framing circle of the dark.
We thought, as she approached, to see her
clearly, but her features only grew more indistinct
as she drew nearer, like those of statues
long submerged in water. We couldn't name her,
she who can't be seen

except in spaces between wars, brief intervals

when history relents, reflection
intervenes, returning home
becomes the epic moment – not the everyday event
postponed in bars; or when you finally reach
the other side of the mountain
and all the paths lead down. As if
an ancient spell had been read backwards:
though what we'd seen – the burning cities
at our backs – had stopped us
in our tracks, a frozen chorus, colonnade
of salt, pillars like the wife of Lot,
the sight of her restored us
to ourselves. How else explain it? The way
she walked among us as we lined her path,
her gaze intent on us till we returned
her look, and then, like embers caught
in a sudden draft, our hope blazed up
again, the flush of blood crept up
reviving limbs…we laughed, embraced,
and were so natural, so like old friends
picking up where we'd left off, it was as if
the interval of stone had gone
from memory, or it had never been.

But the cities *had* burned, the worst
had all been done, was, even now, being done
again – and yet, perhaps…
the one word not at our command: *perhaps*
to learn to live
in the dissolving grip of that green gaze,
put down the shield
emblazoned with the face
of Medusa, the mouth forever open
in a howl. The same face
Goya painted as the rifles were raised
and cocked, *Der Schrei* of Munch
at the vortex where one century of war plunged
into the next; the Pantheon
with its single vacant eye, Cyclops
cramming nations in his mouth –
an emptiness that nothing can assuage
creates its mirror image in
the gaping mouth, unfinished cry
as the head and the body are severed – the horror
on the hero's shield, the sound
of hoofs trampling the wind.

Reading the Bible Backwards

All around the altar, huge lianas
curled, unfurled the dark green
of their leaves to complement the red
of blood spilled there – a kind of Christmas
decoration, overhung with heavy vines
and over them, the stars.
When the angels came, messengers like birds
but with the oiled flesh of men, they hung
over the scene with smoldering swords,
splashing the world when they beat
their rain-soaked wings against the turning sky.

The child was bright in his basket
as a lemon, with a bitter smell from his wet
swaddling clothes. His mother bent
above him, singing a lullaby
in the liquid tongue invented
for the very young – short syllables
like dripping from an eave
mixed with the first big drops of rain
that fell, like tiny silver pears, from
the glistening fronds of palm. The three
who gathered there – old kings uncrowned:
the cockroach, condor, and the leopard, lords
of the cracks below the ground, the mountain
pass and the grass-grown plain – were not
adorned, did not bear gifts, had not
come to adore; they were simply drawn
to gawk at this recurrent, awkward son
whom the wind had said would spell
the end of earth as it had been.

Somewhere north of this familiar scene
the polar caps were melting, the water was
advancing in its slow, relentless
lines, swallowing the old
landmarks, swelling the
seas that pulled
the flowers and the great steel cities down.
The dolphins sport in the rising sea,
anemones wave their many arms like hair
on a drowned gorgon's head, her features
softened by the sea beyond all recognition.

On the desert's edge where the oasis dies
in a wash of sand, the sphinx seems to shift
on her haunches of stone, and the rain, as it runs down,
completes the ruin of her face. The Nile
merges with the sea, the waters rise
and drown the noise of earth. At the forest's
edge, where the child sleeps, the waters gather –
as if a hand were reaching for the curtain
to drop across the glowing, lit tableau.

When the waves closed over, completing the green
sweep of ocean, there was no time for mourning.
No final trump, no thunder to announce
the silent steal of waters; how soundlessly
it all went under: the little family
and the scene so easily mistaken
for an adoration. Above, more clouds poured in
and closed their ranks across the skies;
the angels, who had seemed so solid, turned
quicksilver in the rain.
                        Now, nothing but the wind
moves on the rain-pocked face
of the swollen waters, though far below

where giant squid lie hidden in shy tangles,
the whales, heavy-bodied as the angels,
their fins like vestiges of wings,
sing some mighty epic of their own –

a great day when the ships would all withdraw,
the harpoons fail of their aim, the land
dissolve into the waters, and they would swim
among the peaks of mountains, like eagles
of the deep, while far below them, the old
nightmares of earth would settle
into silt among the broken cities, the empty
basket of the child would float
abandoned in the seaweed until the work of water
unraveled it in filaments of straw,
till even that straw rotted
in the planetary thaw the whales prayed for,
sending their jets of water skyward
in the clear conviction they'd spill back
to ocean with their will accomplished
in the miracle of rain: *And the earth
was without form and void, and darkness
was upon the face of the deep. And
the Spirit moved upon the face of the waters.*

Miriam's Song

Death to the first-born sons, always –
the first fruits to the gods of men.
She had not meant it so, standing in the reeds
back then, the current tugging at her skirt
like hands, she had only meant to save
her little brother, Moses,
red-faced with rage when he was given
to the river. The long curve of the Nile
would keep their line, the promised land
around the bend. Years later
when the gray angel, like the smoke trail
of a dying comet, passed by the houses
with blood smeared over doorways,
Miriam, her head hot in her hands, wept
as the city swelled with the wail of Egypt's women.
Then she straightened up, slowly plaited
her hair and wound it tight around her head,
drew her long white cloak with its deep blue threads
around her, went out to watch the river
where Osiris, in his golden funeral barge,
floated by forever...

as if in offering, she placed a basket on the river,
this time an empty one, without the precious cargo
of tomorrow. She watched it drift a little
from the shore. She threw one small stone in it,
then another, and another, till its weight
was too much for the water and it slowly turned
and sank. She watched the Nile gape and shudder,
then heal its own green skin. She went
to join the others, to leave one ruler
for another, one Egypt for the next.

Some nights you still can see her, by some river
where the willows hang, listening to the heavy tread
of armies, those sons once hidden dark
in baskets, and in her mind she sees her sister,
the black-eyed Pharaoh's daughter, lift the baby
like a gift from the brown flood waters
and take him home to save him, such a pretty
boy and so disarming, as his dimpled hands
reach up, his mouth already open
for the breast.

Minor Epic

The rock where the sword was stuck –
a silver cross that topped the granite,
its business end discreetly buried,
waiting to be hauled out
by a youth, sweet and full of promise
as only legends make them – holds nothing now
but an empty shaft of stone, as vacant
as the dream that the best would rule
when only the worst would want to...

the lake is wise to this, so when
King Arthur, once more dying, tosses in
Excalibur, the arm – as slender and as silver
as a trout – will not be there to catch it,
a feudal hope as broken as
the surface with its spreading rings
to mark the spot the sword has entered
deep, impassive blue. They're sending
divers, rubber-suited and pursued
by bubbles, their anxious faces pressed
to glass, searching for the sword
the lake has taken to its heart
that they will never find
in the mud and murk and weeds
down there, its silver blade impaled
in the lady, neatly nailed
to the bottom of the lake.

Today they're hauling up the *Mary Rose*
from the bottom of the channel, her hold
stuffed with bric-a-brac and bones
of the brave gentlemen of Henry Eight

who took time out from eating
his stupendous roasts to sail
against the French, or rather, watched
from his royal bluff as the *Mary Rose*,
spread-eagled under men and armor, rolled over,
sank like a diving duck in search of dinner
and stayed below for centuries, a spectral
Tudor country weekend party
with its grinning guests. The Prince
of Wales watches as the carcass
lifts above the channel, dripping
things historic – a cable snaps, but the hull
is saved with only a shattered
timber, cannons fire their salute
from a nearby castle, the hulk
is swung on board and brought to shore,
disarmed and rotten, to the cheers
of a little crowd standing
under water, umbrellas raised
beneath the sovereign English rain.

Desert Parable

Miles above them, miles below –
nothing but the heat-stunned air
the hum of insects hovering close
to the tenacious brush that clung
to the canyon wall, the canyon that had been
dry as far back as even the Grandfathers
could remember. Some said the earth
had swallowed the river back, others
that the sky had picked the canyon dry,
hid the river in white sacks
of cloud and carried it to where
the grazing isn't bitter.

She knew the footholds on the cliff
by heart. By day or night, she could pick
her way straight up or down the nicks
cut in the vertical stone. Custom was the purchase
on that rock – only tribal feet could find
their hold and climb the sheer face down
to the pueblo, tucked in the hollow
that time dug in the sandstone wall.
It was the same with hands – the pattern
that your fingers knew, the blankets
woven in the same strict stitch, the zigzag
like the distant lightning flash, until
even in the dark, you could pull the wool across
the tightly strung loom. But she was too restless
to sit with the women and weave; her mind
wandered to another place where the rains fell
thick and sudden like your hair when the combs
are pulled, the teeth of bone let go. And where
the arrows of the sun were broken

by the leaves. Her fingers, following her mind,
lost their place on the taut strings,
tied knots and broke the even rhythms
of the old design. At night, she often called out
in her sleep; by day, picked fights
at the slightest provocation. When the peace
of evening settled on the tribe, her lungs
closed like a fist, she couldn't
breathe; a dark prayer rose
from her – smoke pouring
from a kiva-hole
toward heaven.

At last they drove her from the pueblo up
the sheer cliff to the waiting sky.

By night the men filled in
two of the toeholds, moved
them slightly to the right
so if she tried to climb back
to the village, she would fall
into the endless canyon
of the sky; the buzzards would pick
her bones till they glistened white
as stars. The tribe went back
about its tasks, stolid,
reassured. "She didn't know,"
the old ones said,
"the pueblo is the world."

For the first time that night she slept
without the covering ledge
without the even breathing of the others
in her ears…

just the boundless dark

uninhabited by everything but light

      that drew her till she whirled among the stars
         a pot turned on the great wheel of the sky
until

      in all that burning night

     her own clay seemed to shatter   she felt

a singing in her veins like water   a rush
    of silver that poured out like rain

       and she was lost among

      the galaxies – squash blossoms
      silver   like the necklace of her mother but
       without its weight   so light   it was

     quicksilver   thistledown
       a gleaming river of spilled milk   perhaps

a tongue, a tide of light
      lapping at the shores
          those farther shores
            than night

Sarah's Choice

A little late rain   *The testing*
the desert in the beauty of its winter   *of Sarah*
bloom, the cactus ablaze
with yellow flowers that glow
even at night in the reflected light
of moon and the shattered crystal of sand
when time was so new
that God still walked
among the tents, leaving no prints
in the sand, but a brand burned into
the heart – on such a night
it must have been, although
it is not written in the Book
how God spoke to Sarah
what he demanded of her
how many questions came of it
how a certain faith was
fractured, as a stone is split
by its own fault, a climate of extremes
and one last drastic change
in the temperature.

"Go!" said the Voice. "Take your son,
your only son, whom you love,
take him to the mountain, bind him
and make of him a burnt offering."
Now Isaac was the son of Sarah's age,
a gift, so she thought, from God. And how
could he ask her even to imagine such a thing –
to take the knife
of the butcher and thrust it
into such a trusting heart, then

light the pyre on which tomorrow burns.
What fear could be more holy
than the fear of *that?*

"Go!" said the Voice, Authority's own.
And Sarah rose to her feet, stepped out
of the tent of Abraham to stand between
the desert and the distant sky, holding its stars
like tears it was too cold to shed.
Perhaps she was afraid the firmament
would shudder and give way, crushing her
like a line of ants who, watching
the ants ahead marching safe under the arch,
are suddenly smashed by the heel
they never suspected. For Sarah,
with her desert-dwelling mind, could
see the grander scale in which the heel
might simply be the underside of some Divine
intention. On such a scale, what is
a human son? So there she stood, absurd
in the cosmic scene, an old woman bent
as a question mark, a mote in the eye
of God. And then it was that Sarah spoke
in a soft voice, a speech
the canon does not record.

"No," said Sarah to the Voice.   *The*
"I will not be chosen. Nor shall my son –   *teachings*
if I can help it. You have promised Abraham,   *of Sarah*
through this boy, a great nation. So either
this sacrifice is sham, or else it is a sin.
Shame," she said, for such is the presumption
of mothers, "for thinking me a fool,
for asking such a thing. You must have known
I would choose Isaac. What use have I

for History – an arrow already bent
when it is fired from the bow?"

Saying that, Sarah went into the tent
and found her restless son awake, as if he had
grown aware of the narrow bed in which he lay.
And Sarah spoke out of the silence
she had herself created, or that had been there
all along. "Tomorrow you will be
a man. Tonight, then, I must tell you
the little that I know. You can be chosen
or you can choose. Not both.

"The voice of the prophet grows shrill.
He will read even defeat as a sign
of distinction, until pain itself
becomes holy. In that day, how shall we tell
the victims from the saints,
the torturers from the agents of God?"

"But mother," said Isaac, "if we were not God's
chosen people, what then should we be? I am afraid
of being nothing." And Sarah laughed.

Then she reached out her hand. "Isaac,   *The*
I am going now, before Abraham awakes, before   *unbinding*
the sun, to find Hagar the Egyptian and her son   *of Isaac*
whom I cast out, drunk on pride,
God's promises, the seed of Abraham
in my own late-blooming loins."

"But Ishmael," said Isaac, "how should I greet him?"
"As you greet yourself," she said, "when you bend
over the well to draw water and see your image,
not knowing it reversed. You must know your brother

now, or you will see your own face looking back
the day you're at each other's throats."

She wrapped herself in a thick dark cloak
against the desert's enmity, and tying up
her stylus, bowl, some dates, a gourd
for water – she swung her bundle on her back,
reached out once more toward Isaac.

"It's time," she said. "Choose now."

"But what will happen if we go?" the boy
Isaac asked. "I don't know," Sarah said.

"But it is written   what will happen   if you stay."

Postscript

TO MAXINE KUMIN

Dear Max. I call you that because
two syllables are too much for the sharp
pain your poems cause, the ache
between the shoulder blades, from
what the older centuries called
heart. You're right
and there is something you can do, I can't:
say "I" and "love" and "gone" and
cut it right, neat as a split cord of wood,
the exact heft of the axe,
the straight, swift stroke.

Last week I tried to saw
a dead branch off the fire thorn, and halfway
through I had to stop, not knowing
what I'd do when the damn thing started
falling…standing there, imagining
how it would pull down the power lines,
the wires for the phone, the healthy branch
below, and then, as it tore down
through all the wreckage of those lines
and ruined garden, it would hit me,
its thorns tear through my scalp,
put out my eyes and leave me bleeding
for the neighbors to discover. This sad
and total inability to cut
a simple branch down from the tree
when it was dead a year, this image
like some cheap disaster
film, makes me afraid
of scissors and of saw, of lighting fires,

of using "I," for fear I'll start
some mad striptease of art, tell all,
embarrass everyone, even the dog

and bring the gossip-hounds to sniff
the ruins, the mess I made of it all,
like some baroque explosion in a clean
well-lighted room, and then climb out
onto the windowsill and hoot and
hoot like some demented owl, her feathers
damp from her own rain of tears,
trying to reel back the years – and not the ones
behind, that any fool
would not repeat – but those ahead
that speed up like a train
whose rails I'm tied to
like some poor, abandoned heroine
in a film that everyone is in
so no one wants to see it
over. And yet when you, refusing
both amnesia and the comfort of a myth
can talk as straight as one might
hold a saw to get the dead branch down,
somehow, you save the tree.

While I can't face
the amputation of a branch without
the towers of Troy beginning to go over
like Humpty Dumpty toppling through the years,
his scattered bits the Hittites, the Sumerians,
the Greeks, the Romans (row on row on row),
the French in the deep freeze of the Russian
snow, and don't forget the Jews, the Congolese,
the British Empire shrinking to
tin soldiers on the counterpane

and next America and all that now lives
with her, and then the planet like
a candle sputters out, and the sun
begins to fail in the heavens
and the cold sky fills
with an avalanche of angels, overweight,
falling through their feathers, with
burning hair like figures out of Blake,
and the planets break
their orbits and collide, the firmament
begins to crack and those old waters
that the Fathers said lay just beyond it
pour through the cracks in torrents,
close over everything (except this sonorous
voice-over, this announcer, who seems
to live out universal floods
and still not skip a beat, or miss
a comma) –

            you see, I find myself
in a false position and wish
some sanity would overtake me, like
Don Quijote unhorsed by the Knight
of Mirrors, and just say: dear,
could you just manage
to pull yourself together, take out
the trash and understand the universal
crash is not your business; your flight
from simply stating, from talking straight
as Max, is not being able
to do what Albrecht Dürer did
in just one simple drawing
in his notebook, shortly
before his own untimely death (for
whose death is not untimely?).

It was a portrait of himself, a naked man,
his right arm bent and pointing
at his middle, and written there
below it, just one line,
no easier in German:
"Here, it hurts."

Two Pairs of Eyes

FOR LEAH KOSH

Your eyes are dark and luminous and
mine are not-quite blue or green, depending
on the weather. We alter what we see: you
have the lunar eye and make an opalescent world
of mica chips, translucent fossil wings,
while I, born under the sign of sun, must seek
the glow of light through moving scrims
of gnat-wing, dragonfly. You love the gold leaf
of Byzantium, the sheen of peacock feathers;
I, the autumn sun, gold filtered
through the blazing copper beech.

You turn the snow to silver like the moon
and I regard it with the eye of sun, until
it slips away and swells the rivers.
You paint the stones across the stream
for footing; I always slip
on the slick ones furred with moss
and slide the way a trout does
into shadows. Your ferns are like those pressed
by glaciers into rock, the permanent lace
earth wears beneath her changing skirts
of green. And I, as changeable as dust
on summer paths when the wind lifts it,
will shift the scales of time until
the ferns are huge as trees again and stir
the air with delicate green oars
as if the air were water.

You love blood-red enamel curled inside
the lips of conch, the claws that curve

like new moons at the tips of paws,
the deep luxuriance of fur, the violet impasto
of a royal bruise, the pearls that hatch
from parted lips, and marble eggs licked smooth
by the Aegean, the teeth inside a rose
that tears us with its beauty. And I, why do I
fear these relics with a holy fear?

For while shells build the glory of
a coral reef, I feel the crumbling
sand beneath my feet, torn out by tide.
I send what shells I find to you, dear friend
and astral eye, I who cannot read the bones
nor prophesy. These mysteries are not mine.
I gather shells for you, for love
but as I do, I cry – for what art cannot do,
no more can I; I turn and watch the tide.
It moves the shells in the glitter of the foam
almost, almost I say
as if they were alive.

"Never Apologize for Poetry"

FOR MY STUDENTS

Despite the times, the tedious self,
the global crimes – there is still music
in the leaves and magic in the cunning
spiral of a snail, and falling water
with its lovely, ruinous cascade of sound,
all this that beggars speech and yet
gives tongue. And when we say, "I, too, hate
poetry," it is not modesty forbids
the brag of art, but this abundant
wily earth our words must fail. Yet
in this union with the word, the long reach
of our little minds that compass
galaxies and quail before the corners
of a room at night, can still
ignite what otherwise might just go
        darkly
                on
as a fox deep in the hedgerow
brings its eyes to light
the otherwise too blank a green
and gazing out, gives its bright
sentience to the opacity of leaves –
though here the trope must fail before
the fox, who suddenly gets up, swerves out
of our conceit to go its own
unhuman way, and yet the last
red blaze of tail, defiant plume
that waves off in the closing grass, turns back
into an emblem of our concealment,
red flag to warn the others off, meanwhile
our eyes will go on burning, stay

when all the world goes on its accidental
artful way – a double vision
bright inside the hedge, nature
given memory and pause…

as sun pays homage to the solid world
by laying shadows at its feet, as sky
lies looking up from the reflecting ponds
and clouds rest easily among
the lily pads, the sky and water, blue
and green, are so at one
that those two realms they say the gods
divided at the start, are mixed again
along these shaded paths, so far
from war, where leaves command
their ancient speech and falling water
telling its passage in the hand
has its own cool blue renewed
by touching us, the spell is cast
and joyful and assured
of our defeat, we spell it back
(*adieu*) into another hand.

Classical Proportions of the Heart

FOR FONTAINE

Everyone here knows how it ends, in the stone
amphitheater of the world, everyone
knows the story – how Jocasta
in her chamber hung herself for shame
how Oedipus tore out his eyes and stalked
his darkened halls crying
aaiiee   *aaiiee*   woe   woe is me   woe

These things everyone expects, shifting
on the cold stone seats, the discomfort
of our small, hard place in things
relieved by this public show of agony;
how we love this last bit best, the wait
always worth it: the mask with its empty eyes,
the sweet sticky horror of it all,
the luxurious wailing, the release,
the polis almost licking its lips,
craning our necks to make out the wreck –
the tyrant brought low, howling,
needing at last to lean
on a mere daughter, Antigone, who
in the sequel will inherit
her father's flair for the dramatic,
her mother's acquaintance with death;
her hatred of falsehood, her own.

We feel a little superior, our seats
raised above the circle where the blinded
lion paces out his grief, self-condemned,
who could not keep his mastery to the end
(so Creon taunts him). What a flush
of pleasure stains our faces then

at the slow humiliation of an uncommon man
a Classical Golgotha without God, only
an eyeless wisdom, Apollo useless
against age, guilt, bad temper
and, most of all, against Laius
whose fear twisted the oracle's tongue,
child-hater, the father who started it all.

The same night, as the howls rose
from the palace of Oedipus, the crowd
rising, drawing on their cloaks to go home,
far from the stage, that dramatic circle
that fixed our gaze, out there
on the stony hills gone silver under the moon
in the dry Greek air, the shepherd sits
he who saved the baby from the death
plotted by Laius, he who disobeyed a king
for pity's sake. Sitting there alone
under the appalling light of the stars
what does he think of how the gods
have used him, used his kind heart
to bait the trap of tragedy?
What brief can he make for mercy
in a world that Laius rules?

Sitting there, the moon his only audience,
perhaps he weeps, perhaps he feels
the planetary chill alone out there
on what had been familiar hills.
Perhaps he senses still the presence
of the Sphinx. And maybe
that is when he feels the damp
nudge against his hand.
By reflex, we could guess, he reaches out
to touch the coat of wool, begins

to stroke the lamb. "It's late," he says
at last, and lifts the small beast
to his chest, carrying it down
the treacherous stony path toward home, holding
its warmth against him. There is little drama
in this scene, but still its pathos has
a symmetry, because the lamb's small heat
up close exactly balances
the distant icy stars,
and when it senses home, and bleats,
its small cry weighs against
the wail of fallen kings.
There is, as well, the perfect closure
as the shepherd's gate swings shut
and a classical composure
in the way he bears
the burden of his heavy heart
with ease.

II.

Beauty and the Beast

Her fur new-licked, the whitetail fawn
peers wide-eyed through the screen
of field grass, her ears outspread
to catch the slightest sound. Even asleep,
her ears are pricked and ready, as if
to catch intruders in her dreams.
But breathe her name, she's gone.

"These things in which we have seen
ourselves and spoken" turn from us now;
even the rocks, in which we glimpsed
enduring things, obscure themselves,
perhaps deliberately, in mist.
As deer, when caged in zoos or
put to other abstract uses,
lose their thick plush of russet
brown, the wetness of their
noses, their special way of stopping
at a sound – so when we fling our net
of thought, the living silver
of the ocean clots. To what
pass have we come, when hope
is no more than desire
to share in their oblivion,
when what seemed brute and dumb
till we had loaned it beauty's
tongue, seems now as eloquent
as silent heaven?

We, who burned our brand
into the uncomplaining flank
of the creation, begin to hope

for what may yet survive us...
and as the animals grow
smaller, moving off into a blue, inhuman
distance, we dare not call out
after them: "Good luck!"
for fear our best-meant words, straight
from the heart, will follow them
as they depart, and curse them.

The Last Man

FOR VIVIAN SCHATZ

Here, in our familiar streets, the day
is brisk with winter's business.
The reassuring rows of brick façades,
litter baskets overflowing
with the harvest of the streets
and, when the light turns, the people
move in unison, the cars miraculously
slide to a stop, no one is killed,
the streets, for some reason, do not
show the blood that is pouring
like a tide, on other shores.

    Martinez, the last peasant left alive
    in his village, refuses to run, hopes
    that God, *El Salvador*,
    will let him get the harvest in.
    "Can a fish live out of water?" he says
    for why he stays, and weeds
    another row, ignoring the fins
    of sharks that push up
    through the furrows.

Here, it is said, we live
in the belly of the beast. Ahab sits
forever at the helm, his skin
white wax, an effigy. The whale carries
him, lashed to its side by the ropes
from his own harpoon. His eyes
are dead. His ivory leg
juts from the flank of Leviathan
like a useless tooth.

One more time, the distant sail appears,
a cloud forms, an old icon for mercy
turned up in a dusty corner
of the sky, preparing rain
for the parched land, Rachel
weeping for her children. "Can a fish
live out of water?" he asks
and the rain answers, in Spanish,
manitas de plata
little hands of silver on his brow.

The American Sublime: Robert Penn Warren

High in the mountain pass, tucked in a crevice
of stone, the eagle's nest throbs
with its naked young, open-mouthed and crying
to be fed. The eagle soars, the voice
of the wind in the highest pines
doesn't whine; it sounds,
to a human ear, like sobbing.

Old man, we say you're too rhetorical and
too sublime, as if an eagle when it spread
wide wings and rode the cold wind
down the mountain pass, its great yellow eye
wide open, could be other than it is.

Below, deep in the years, a boy
and his husky, *Sila*, a ruin of stonework,
a blank sheet of snow: there
for the billionth time since the earth
begat, and the cells moved in their unknowing,
mindful way toward flesh and fur, the dog
leaped at the doe's throat and the snow
blossomed red as a bridal
sheet – the doe torn, the dog
docile again, stained crimson
on its silver muzzle, confused
by the pain on its master's face, himself
armed for the kill. And you, that boy
grown old, the taste of blood
still fresh from the knife that cut short
the death throes of the deer, the blood still
warm on the blade after so many years, unable
to make it right, to make it fit without

the bite of the saw-wheel, tooth on tooth, turning
as the planet turns, the sun staining the sky
with red, the snow falling again
in useless white denial.

We, who say the word
ecology as if it were God, accuse you
of the orator's sin, you
who looked long and long into the cold
blue eyes of the husky and
the warm brown eyes of the doe –
and wept, and cried out…what words
without the rhetorical sweep
like the wide-open wings of the eagle
riding the cold current at the top of the pass
could do it justice, this world
without justice or help
for the heart, beating
like the helpless young in their nest
crying for the sky-driven beak, seeing, at last,
the great bird coming like love
down over them, bringing death in its beak
to comfort them, and the huge darkness
of itself, like love, for cover
against the cold galactic night.

Tucson Gardens

ON THE ARIZONA PHOTOGRAPHS OF WILLIAM LARSON

The wagon trails stopped here, ditched
at the desert's edge. Fish left this ocean
long ago to sand. Here only the wind speaks
Spanish, and, at the edge of town, the ghosts
of conquistadors blow, light as tumbleweed
across dry ground. The green here is sad,
it lives on artificial rain, sprinklers and
long vinyl serpents of the human host –
fence-builder, who answers the tangle of dry
vine, the palm's shaggy explosion of fronds,
the riot of the nerves, the intricate curves
of the wild – with the plumb line,
the cube of cement, the grid of the mind.

Our time, held still in the cool gaze of the lens,
a chemical fix, the shutter poised
under your finger like a trigger –
nothing moves. This is the suburb,
stubborn, the gardens of us temporary gods.
Out there, the mountains are a line
drawn on a graph, a record
of the rise and fall of unrecorded time.

There is desert out there, pal,
and here, the placid battle lines are drawn –
chainlinks, trellis, and the picket fence
make their last stand. The hand, if it were
freed, if it reached out and touched,
would bleed, the cactus bristling
like a porcupine, the garden of thorns,
the cypress like the feathers

of dead Indians, guardians
at the edge of open land.

But what most strongly haunts this place
is us, a strange nostalgia
for the present.
How else explain the careful emptiness,
the unkempt cultivation of a place
both occupied, deserted – abandoned
Arizona of the heart, where
we are missing
in the middle of our lives.

How else explain, in a place so dry, the
soft watercolor wash of sky,
the pale green, as if we thinned
our palette with our tears.
How else explain the quality of light
that turns the otherwise familiar scene
to the hand-tinted postcards of a dream,
a gentler time, pasted in an album
on a shelf. Here, where the west begins
to end – regret, the empty
garden seat, the yucca
like a dried bouquet
of bayonets, the thorny hedge
defends the secret houses
where we hide, wounded birds
who dream of flight
alone and exiled
in our nests.

High Noon at Los Alamos

To turn a stone
with its white squirming
underneath, to pry the disc
from the sun's eclipse – white heat
coiling in the blinded eye: to these malign
necessities we come
from the dim time of dinosaurs
who crawled like breathing lava
from the earth's cracked crust, and swung
their tiny heads above the lumbering tons
of flesh, brains no bigger than a fist
clenched to resist the white flash
in the sky the day the sun-flares
pared them down to relics for museums,
turned glaciers back, seared Sinai's
meadows black – the ferns withered, the swamps
were melted down to molten mud, the cells
uncoupled, recombined, and madly
multiplied, huge trees toppled to the ground,
the slow life there abandoned hope,
a caterpillar stiffened in the grass.
Two apes, caught in the act of coupling,
made a mutant child
who woke to sunlight wondering, his mother
torn by the huge new head
that forced the narrow birth canal.

As if compelled to repetition
and to unearth again
white fire at the heart of matter – fire
we sought and fire we spoke,
our thoughts, however elegant, were fire

from first to last – like sentries set to watch
at Argos for the signal fire
passed peak to peak from Troy
to Nagasaki, triumphant echo of the burning
city walls and prologue to the murders
yet to come – we scan the sky
for that bright flash,
our eyes stared white from watching
for the signal fire that ends
the epic – a cursed line
with its caesura, a pause
to signal peace, or a rehearsal
for the silence.

As Far as it Goes, and Back

Tearing through the lovely landscape
of Honshu – its brief perfections – the bullet
train cutting them short,
boring through mountain after mountain,
black shaft driven
through the deep volcanic night
then breaking out, for a held breath
into the sun, a flash of green fields
flooded with water, half-filled with sky –
then back to the black again.

Those green, happy valleys
out of a child's book, like bright
spaces between the words in a sentence
whose meaning is dark – tunnel
after tunnel, all I can see of the heart
of Japan, except for the brief blaze
of green against the glass – those tall young
mountains in their pointed sorcerers' hats
of tufted green velvet, the nestled farms,
each roof with its curling lift
of wings at the outer edge, ready
at the first tremor of earth
to fly…how easily it all
slips by, slips back

to a bright memory,
a never-never land, seen only
as lost children see, wandering
in time, the sudden reflection
of a mother in the mirror –

as bright and reassuring,
as quickly gone.

Then back in the tunnel again,
forced back inside the stubborn heart
on the bullet train of the years
hurtling through the darkness
of an old and foreign night, a tunnel
where – however brightly lit the car
in which you sit, bragging of awareness
to others as preoccupied as you –
out there, behind the pane, nothing is
revealed; regression into dark and loss,
and staring blankly back
your own estranged, familiar face
congealed in speeding glass.

Nandin's Tail

FOR SUJATA

As the sun comes up on the suffering world
the stone gods writhe along the twisted
columns on the temple wall, a cliff
the weather sculpted with its hundred tongues.
Within, a blunt stone phallus prods
the blue dusk of the inner shrine, while
at its door, adoring, Nandin, the sweet
devoted cow-eyed Brahma bull, kneels
worshipping the power throbbing
     in the Shiva-stone.
And everywhere, the eyes – black as
watermelon seeds, as countless.

While double-natured Shiva dances
along the colonnades of whirling cosmic dust
comets streaming from his outspread hair,
the galaxies a storm of gnats,
deep in the cow-mind of Nandin, a different
figure wanders, losing herself
among the thick and dripping leaves,
enormous as the ears of elephants, until
it isn't clear
which is forest shadow and which
her darkening shape. Shiva exhales a last
exhausted breath, lies down among
the ruined worlds he has unmade, strands
of his torn hair like rivers tangled
in his hands, the planets smashed like berries
on the moss below his still white form.

With a racket of bones, her necklace
of skulls swinging over her hanging breasts
Kali leaps and pounds the inert god,
her feet pestles of brass, her laughter
rattling in her throat like dry seeds
in a gourd. And Shiva stirs, his pallor
brightens, his belly fills with air.
He rises as the double-god again, he whose other
half is woman; blue-breasted maiden
on the right; left side, a youth whose beard
is just beginning. It all comes round again –
the slow dance of the planets, the great wheel
humming in the sky, the rivers
spreading toward the sea
as the uncoiling cobra spreads its hood and hisses
rising toward the red-soaked altar
of the dawn.

I shake my head and wish it all
away – the tail of Nandin swishing
to brush off flies – and listen
to the whisper of the maple leaves
stirring at the glass, the rush
of passing cars, the comforting hiss
of tires on concrete – and listening so
to what is close, I miss
the clang of worlds colliding
resounding brass beyond our little reach,
cymbals
in what we only dream
are hands.

The Towers of Silence

Lost with the sun in a chartreuse wood, afflicted
by associations, flies, thirst, and by
a growing chill my clothes cannot keep
out, the path narrowing as I go
like a road in a Roethke poem, taking you out
that long peninsula, the one with the snow, the sand, the ruts
in which your wheels stick
while the headlights darken, flicker and go out...

though without a vehicle
and going on foot, I know those roads
today, on the brightest day of early
winter, when the sun makes much of the few
gold leaves still clinging to the branch
as if setting an example
that one could attain, with the slightest
effort, a great cheerfulness –
nevertheless, it is then
that the road starts to narrow
and the sides, closing in, are lined
with something dark like stands of evergreen
but with the hard reflective sheen of polished
stone, like the shining black marble walls
of the Vietnam monument, where, hard as you
strain to understand, you see nothing
but your own face reflected back
scarred with the names
of the dead.

2.

And now the towers of silence rise
as if the dead-end path had suddenly
turned and opened on a vast landscape
of sand where silent towers wait, circled
by birds, endlessly circled.
Far out on such a wide, bleached plain
the merciful Zoroastrians raise
their towers, so high the silence
dominates the plain. Up there
they place their dead, the bodies
exposed on platforms
against a vacancy of blue,
and leave them for the birds.

Uncanny, those towers standing so aloof
so silent with their ruined cargo
from a voyage that is past, and the birds
too high and far away for us to hear
their cries; there is only the slow
inexorable orbit of appetite,
centripetal, as if each bird were tied
by invisible string
to the protractor of some immense
geometer, the sharply drawn circle of
the buzzard, condor, kite.

3.

"Stay with the body,"
the last morality out here
where the West begins, high
in the mountain pass, where the cold will keep
the body till the rescue comes. "Stay

with the body." Though the chill deepens
and duty, that binds us here, makes us
harder and harder to tell
from what we guard, slowly being covered
by the kindness of snow, like Antigone's
deliberate scattering of the dust of Thebes
to preserve the form of a beloved
brother. Yet, as the play unfolds
and even as she argues with the king,
the dogs and birds, like messengers
from an older god, disturb the dust, begin
the slow dispersal of Polynices
through the polis, fragments
taken to the altars and the hearths
and while she bids her bridal hopes farewell,
the human body – centered in the circle
like Leonardo's famous figure on the rack
of art – is slowly torn apart. And while
she leaves the light behind forever, you can hear
the cries of birds almost like triumph,
the snarling of the dogs in argument
over what each one will have.

4.

Out toward the periphery
at the border of what is bearable
where detachment rules,
the Towers of Silence stand.
Now, on those platforms the past is being
picked clean, purified by air and
distance, for it all happens at such a height,
so far away – it could be Plato's dream:
a perfect circle in the sky – except
it moves, it turns, and so shifts to another

text, becomes the wheel of Heraclitus
the transformation of a cast-off flesh
into the winged messengers
of change. And I wonder

if after the magical three days
when the platforms are empty, the birds
risen from the dead and flown, the circle
broken, nothing left but the brilliant
white bones, the sky stripped
of everything but blue –
if with a sigh or a shudder
of release, the watchers turn away, anxious
to move on, climb on their kneeling camels,
feel the strange, humped flesh
back under them as it gathers itself up and,
like a minor earthquake, its hills
lurch, shudder and lift, the horizon
suddenly shifting – then they're off
in that wild pitch and roll
of the camel's gait on sand,
growing smaller and smaller, unless

here, we decide to go with them
because they carry their own water
because the land is dry, the sun hot
and our need for company acute
when, from our own silent towers,
we come down alive.

It's Not Cold Here

FOR BOB

Somewhere the flags are frozen
in the bitter wind and cannot flap,
the brittle trees stand outlined in the ice,
black relics in glass cases, backlit
by the sickly light of a fitful sun;
somewhere the drifts of snow are studded
with those who didn't make it home,
who died embedded in the white
where they sought cover; somewhere water
falling slow over the stone rift
in the mountain, froze solid
and hangs in air like some perfected dogma…

but it's not cold here
although outside it's winter –
this place we never chose, but only
found, as luck would have it,
as mountain streams, impetuous and cold,
flow down but with no way of knowing
how slow they'd grow and brown
on broad alluvial plains.
Too much is made of choice:
we merely came the way we could
being what we were, and we were changed
by the terrain we came by. Nor could we
see around a single bend
until we'd turned it. And it was wind
and not a course we'd charted
that brought us to a pebbled shore
whose stones the sea had shaped and
polished, and gave us food we'd never

tasted. Of this, we had no premonition
nor even, quite, desire;
though we may dream of fire
when lost in ice, the temperate zones
are never those we dream of, the mind
proceeding by extremes, desire by contrast.

And now it's hard to say just where we are
except it isn't cold here,
the light is often amber,
we can't remember
the sting of wind-whipped snow
against the eyes nor the stop-frame
of the ice. Here we are happy,
forgetful of the cold – as well-fed children,
dragging sleds, see every snowbound hill
as heaven, made just to climb
for the pure abandoned joy of sliding down.

"*Midway the journey of this life…*"

FOR VICKY

we reach a place without a border
on the past, for no one
walks here hot with hate
trying to unwind her soul
from the sharp spindle of childhood
when she was held
by other hands, and spun and twisted
on the narrow stick. Here
there is a slow turning in a bright air,
but it is not that counterspin
with which we all begin. Not now. Not anymore.
Nor is this nostalgia's realm
whose citizens keep stumbling into what is lost,
regrets half-buried in the grass,
so every forward step is a little turning back.

No. Here the place itself is ancient
beyond our count, deep in that other history
of trees, their roots sunk under walls
until they pull them down, leaving
a scatter of stones, as if some epic
game were interrupted, the pieces dropped
in the grass, and the point mislaid.
For everyone but the simple
and the wise, who never saw the point, forgot
what the wall was for,
though many brought their stones to it
and the small mortar of their hopes.

Now, where so much is undisclosed,
there is suggestion in the air, a stir

so light it moves us, for we are
airy now as a veil of lace,
sheer enough for the light
to pass straight through, as if we were
no thicker than our skins.

And the scattered stones, strewn here
and there, no longer can be called
ruins – the dying fall of such a word demands
desire for a past that stands
still between us and the sun.
The stones instead seem the runes
of grass, some arcane statement
that the field is making.

As a seed that's winged
with soft white down is borne aloft,
it neither seeks the ground nor thinks
of growing, it is the most abandoned, freest
thing, it floats the way
wind veers and may land anywhere,
take root, or simply rot.
Mere bits of breathing, downy stuff,
so many, such a multitude – the earth
will catch enough of us to make a spring,
while those blown down on water or on sand
will decorate the surface like a snow,
dress all the world in momentary lace,
so whether we end
in use, we end in beauty, moved as if
in trance, the flight has stirred us and
the open air become a scroll
for the slow, unwinding spiral of our dance.

The Green Connection

IN CELEBRATION OF TRUDY AND MIKE

When the vein of jade is opened
in the spring, winter's icy hasp
pried loose – the lid comes off the universe
of carp, just where the sun is looking
with its long warm gaze of gold
the frozen vein begins to flow again
as a line of song, learned by heart as a child,
forgotten for years, runs again
in the mind, the melting jade
begins to slide, crowding its shores
spreading out, starting to pour
down the long, falling curve
of the young mountain, filling
as it goes, a long green song of water
recalling itself, as a scroll of fern
unrolls in the first spring sun, turning
the hard rock of the heights
into a lyrical passage, light moving
through shade into waiting –
the rains expected soon,
the rice paddies will fill again,
the squares of mud become mirrors
sprouting green, as if reflection
on its own could grow, as if the sky
had come to rest down here
and in between, the shoots of green that grow
from what has been to what will be

the grains of rice
whose polish and the steam
make them glisten in the bowl

the delicate white of porcelain, rice paper
shoji screens, each square aglow
with light, shine like pearls in water
back home, night's black impasto
scraped off by the flat palette knife
of dawn, a pair of shutters
suddenly thrown wide, and from
the open window at the center of the man
a woman leans out, calling
to the brightening day
and sees a pair of white cranes float
across the miles of sky, across
the frame of the painter's eye, to where
the snow is still thick on the peaks of
Asagai, while in our garden here in
Hatsudai, the rough and twisted trunk
succumbs to spring, and overnight
unfolds its bridal silks
of plum.

TOKYO, 1986

Conversation with a Japanese Student

That lovely climbing vine, so fresh
at dawn, so shy at noon, whose blue
countenance we call Morning Glory, you
call it *asakao*, Morning Face.
"What is this glory," you ask, child
of *akarui*, even the memory of war
effaced. "What is it all *for?*"

⌒

Here is an artist working, his brush
is history's tongue, his canvas
allegorical and large, the landscape
must be ample for his theme –
the turn of epic tides, pulled
in the wake of a dream. Glory,
unlike her homely twin, Mortality,
casts no shadow, never rests
("A beautiful and charming Female
Floating Westward through the air,
bearing on her forehead
the Star of Empire"). There,

notice that Glory is artfully draped
in a tunic of pale silk in the Classical style
her limbs as plump and supple
as oil paint and appetite
can make them, the lift of her head – proud,
a summons and a dare, one delicious arm
carries a bright banner streaming in the air
its design illegibly wrought
with large suggestions. But of Glory
you can be sure because

an army marches in her train –
almost a shadow, darkening the land.
At times, a peasant woman
raising her gaunt baby in a trite appeal
may momentarily block the light, obscure
Glory, put a little in the shade
all that golden beauty
the toss of whose curls is worth
a thousand ships, a million
villages, the world

for even a glimpse, the faintest rustle
of the hem of Beatrice's skirt
as it disappears around the corner
of those gates of pearl to the eternal
harbor, the flutter of doves
in the white thighs of Helen, desire
in its perfected form. The mirror of art
becomes a burning glass in the light
of absolute desire, the brush a flame
about to be consumed, for he has reached
the limits, here, of art – as Michelangelo
one night when he was old, in his rage
at the stubborn stone's refusal
to yield to his conception, attacked
his last Pietà with his chisel
trying to tear the pattern from the matter,
Christ from the arms of his grieving
mother; his servant
was forced to subdue the master
in order to save the work.

This time, no servant soul to intervene
and fire at the core, the center
split – as if mankind, with its cold

forever mind, trapped in its furious, failing heart
had torn the Pietà apart from within – gone
the mother, a cloud of glowing dust,
gone the son, dissolved
in the monstrous cloud, heaven's fungus
growing on the axis of the world
casting its white shadow on the hills
pitiless as any parasite
whose life depends
on what it slowly kills.

No brush can paint a light so pure
    only the blind can see   white hot
   it whites out everything but what is not
      the sun's high noon, but brighter...

"ex Occidente, lex; ex Oriente, lux"
    out of the West, law; out of the East, light.

  ∽

At Nagasaki in the Peace Park near
the epicenter of the blast
there is a glade
so dense with foliage, bushes, *asakao*
and pine, you'd almost miss the sign, hand-drawn,
the only one in English that I saw:

THEY SAID NOTHING WOULD GROW HERE
  FOR 75 YEARS

And though the language was my own
I found it difficult to read
through such a thick exquisite screen
of evergreen
and tears.

Having Eaten of the Tree of Knowledge

On the plains of Thessaly
where the wheat had begun again
its season, a fresh wind tore
the wreath of clouds from Mount Olympus,
the sun picked out the peak of naked rock
and kindled it. The horses grazing
placid in green pastures, looked up
with liquid eyes as fathomless as dreams
and though we'll never know
it was as if they might have thought
of Chiron, wise centaur, wounded
by his half that was the human,
who traded his Olympian situation,
the immortality of gods and
monsters, for death
to heal an old division.

So we come down from stony haunts –
the hypothetical eternal – to find another
way into the garden, not by the gate
guarded by the iron angel. Nor shall we
call it by the ancient name. After so long
an exile, what have we to do with Edens?
Bred on the bitter fruit of choice, having
soaked the earth with the dragon's blood
pouring from our mortal wounds –
this time we'll pick the other Tree
and eat the fruit of life.

FROM *Shekhinah* (1984)

I.

Emigration

There are always, in each of us,
these two: the one who stays,
the one who goes away –
Charlotte, who stayed in the rectory
and helped her sisters die in England;
Mary Taylor who went off to Australia
and set up shop with a woman friend.
"Charlotte," Mary said to her, "you are all
like potatoes growing in the dark."
And Charlotte got a plaque in Westminster
Abbey; Mary we get a glimpse of
for a moment, waving her kerchief
on the packet boat, and disappearing.
No pseudonym for her, and nothing
left behind, no trace
but a wide wake closing.

Charlotte stayed, and paid and paid –
the little governess with the ungovernable
heart, that she put on the altar.
She paid the long indemnity of all
who work for what will never wish them well,
who never set a limit to what's owed
and cannot risk foreclosure. So London
gave her fame, though it could never
sit comfortably with her at dinner –
how intensity palls when it is
plain and small and has no fortune.

When she died with her unborn child
the stars turned east
to shine in the gum trees of Australia,

watching over what has sidetracked evolution,
where Mary Taylor lived
to a great old age, Charlotte's letters in a box
beside her bed, to keep her anger hot.

God bless us everyone until we sicken, until
the soul is like a little child
stricken in its corner by the wall; so there is
one who always sits there under lamplight
writing, staying on, and one
who walks the strange hills of Australia,
far too defiant of convention for the novels
drawn daily from the pen's "if only" –
if only Emily had lived,
if only they'd had money, if only
there had been a man who'd loved them truly…
when all the time there had been
Mary Taylor, whom no one would remember
except she had a famous friend named Charlotte
with whom she was so loving-angry,
who up and left to take her chances
in that godforsaken outpost past
the reach of fantasy, or fiction.

Without Regret

Nights, by the light of whatever would burn:
tallow, tinder and the silken rope
of wick that burns slow, slow
we wove the baskets from the long gold strands
of wheat that were another silk: worm soul
spun the one, yellow seed in the dark soil, the other.

The fields lay fallow, swollen with frost,
expectant winter. Mud clung to the edges
of our gowns; we had hung back like shadows
on the walls of trees and watched. In the little circles
that our tapers threw, murdered men rose red
in their clanging armor, muttered
words that bled through the bars
of iron masks: *the lord*
who sold us to the glory fields, lied.

Trumpets without tongues, we wove lilies
into the baskets. When they asked us
what we meant by these, we'd say "mary, mary"
and be still. We lined the baskets on the sill
in the barn, where it is always dusk
and the cows smell sweet. Now the snow

sifts through the trees, dismembered
lace, the white dust of angels, angels.
And the ringing of keys that hang
in bunches at our waists, and the sound of silk
whispering, whispering.
There is nothing in the high windows
but swirling snow,

the glittering milk of winter.
The halls grow chill. The candles flicker.
Let them wait who will and think what they want.
The lord has gone with the hunt, and the snow,
the snow grows thicker. Well he will keep
till spring thaw comes. Head, hand, and heart –
baskets of wicker, baskets of straw.

Eleusis

FACTS: March 6. Marianne Bachmeier, a barmaid, walked
into a Lubeck courtroom, fired six shots and killed Klaus
Grabowski, 35, accused of molesting and strangling her
7-year-old daughter. Grabowski had a long criminal
record, including sex offenses against young girls. In 1973
he received a year's probation after trying to strangle a
6-year-old girl. In 1975 a judge, after finding him guilty
of sexually molesting two 9-year-olds, sent him to a
psychiatric hospital for a year. Marianne Bachmeier,
daughter of a member of Hitler's Waffen-SS, is waiting
to be tried for murder. The West German Sunday paper,
Bild am Sonntag, called her, in a headline, "Mother
Marianne."

The Law. The majesty of Law. "We are only
following orders."

In the countryside, where the crops are not yet
seeded in the ground, the earth shudders –
it opens yet another time, yawns
in some rapt exhaustion, and once again, in a swirl
of gravel, the sound of hoofs on stone,
the ruler rides, brother to the high god, Dis –
claiming the first flowers of the earth
he has divided. The land groans, and the women
weep, as they have always wept, as
the Father consents, the judges agree, the psychiatrists
nod their heads wisely and note
in German phrases in their little spiral books:
"He could not help himself; he had, no doubt,
a bad mother, an unresolved Oedipal complex.
Commit him to our care, and we shall set him free."

Crushed flowers in the wheel-rut on the road.
The voice of Hera coming down the years:
*"If I cannot prevail upon the high gods,
I will stir up Hell."* The clouds close in,
the light is strange and violet, almost
a bruise; Demeter tears her dark veil, tears
her long corn-colored hair, and stirs
the blood of Marianne, bearer of the cup,
the tarnished chalice, mother, murderess.
In her dreams, her little girl cries out,
cries out…the cry is endless as
the wars the Law allows: the vineyards
forever trampled under boots, the rumble
of the tanks replacing plows, the roar
of the chariot of Dis. He has split
the earth, the atom, the heart
of the world cracks –
and the petals look like scraps of silk
scattered in the dust. *Rape:* Old French
for the split skins and the stalks of grapes
after the wine has been pressed out.

And we were taught in school
how Roman law (and legions) brought
the world under a single rule; how
Greek men brought us closer to the sun,
the rule of light, annulling
the rule of blood for the pure, uneasy balance
of the Law. They blinded her – old Justice
with her bandaged eyes; set her, impartial, into stone
before the doors of courts, and sent
the Furies back, back into their caves
into the blood-red recess of the heart,
where they could only howl and tear
at their own flesh – no more to steal

the sleep of men or hound the killers
of their own kin and kind
until they fell upon the altars, spilled
like so much wine. So Death rode with the Law,
conscription took the young, and Justice,
in her marble robes, muttered *Pace, Pace,*
under her breath, and war led on to more,
death wholesale and life cheap; the buzzards
grew fat, more certain of their meat. Only
their necks, loose folds of hanging flesh, betrayed
them. The land put off the wearing of the green.

With a tearing sound, so like the tearing
of a young girl's flesh, Justice tears off her blindfold,
steps down from her perch of stone, her limbs
grow warm again, the live blood pulsing
through the marble veins…and Mother
Marianne loads her gun: six bullets, one
for each of the pomegranate seeds
that stained her daughter's mouth
with red. She throws her weight against
the courtroom doors, bursts in – burning
like a torch, a brand in the hand of Demeter –
and fires six shots at Klaus before the eyes
of a stunned court, and the children there
on an outing for their civics class.

*"I sing of Demeter, the lovely haired, and of
her daughter, Kore, slender ankled, picking flowers
by the lake, and singing…"*

Zeus gave her to his brother for his sport.
The time grows short; the wounds of earth are
gaping. Sisters, brothers, light
your torches and restore

the mysteries. The wheat is all the gold
we'll ever know, the earth our own, and only
sphere. A deeper law moves scarlet in its veins.
We are but nature given eyes, and by a twist
of DNA, earth given to our care.
As old men rage in all our capitals,
as the missiles shuttle on their tracks,
earth shudders and Persephone
is rising in the fields, and all the flowers –
as if the dumb, dishonored earth were given tongues –
cry out, cry out, cry out.

The World is Not a Meditation

Odysseus, Penelope
that aging wife with a fixed idea – Odysseus.
Strange pair to put against the blare of sirens
on the news, prime-time wars that flicker
through the brain – still, through it all:
one man lashed to a mast, one woman
tied by her own hair to a loom.

She nods a little at her work, her hands
fall idle in her lap. By now, she isn't sure
what she is waiting for; her mind
wanders, she has stopped
trying to comb the knots from her hair
nights, when the candles sputter
like some bright notion she's about
to lose. His seed is scattered
in so many nymphs, it's no surprise
that half the babies born
on distant islands look like him,
though they think different thoughts and
cannot bear his name. The son he spawned
in legal loins is out for him, inheritor
of his mother's fond obsession. The others
turn away from him, without a blink
of recognition – black eyes, exactly
his, black as the ripe olives
pressed for oil, that endless flow
that keeps the great wheels wet
and turning, cutting grooves across the back
of earth; everywhere, the burning towns.

Odysseus has returned. And the men
who sailed with him? All lost
or drowned. He's stopped his ears
so he won't hear them calling, men
tossed into the waves like coins
to appease some hypothetical Poseidon.
Their sound keeps breaking
on the shore – the voices of the drowned,
the unrenowned, the living tide
incessant, whispering: anonymous,
anonymous, anonymous…the foam
left on the stones when the waves
withdraw – transparent roe, ghost spawn,
it glitters for a moment and is gone.

It is the morning after
Odysseus' return. The suitors lie in heaps
like so much garbage, the flies
already thick. Outside the great gate
of his house on Ithaca, a wailing
like a siren call – the women
with their urns, empty, asking
for the ashes of their sons, their lovers,
something – even a word.
But the shutters of the great house stay closed
against the hot Greek sun. The women
turn at last and go, to glean
the fields, to make strange beds, whatever
kind of home they can invent.
Only Penelope holds her own man
in her arms, the man who left her
to her own thoughts all those years.
What she thinks now
is hers alone, Odysseus the intruder.

For those who don't like endings, let the story lift
like ruffled feathers in the wind,
refuse to settle. And let
the not-quite fiction of Penelope
pick up another thread from deep inside her
where the nerves are taut along the bone,
her body like the lute when it is strummed,
from a house that's full
of signals: the slow foot of the cat
upon the stair, the roaches drinking
in the pipes, the hairs that seem to swim
in the washing water, the lizards
rustling in the leaves, the way
that even silence is alive
with premonitions.

Listen. The sound of scissors clicking.
One by one, she cuts the threads
that strung the loom. The shroud
that she'd been weaving
becomes a cloud of falling
shreds, till the room is littered
with useless threads, like sentences
from which the sense has fled.
She shakes her head as if to free it
from the name that she'd repeated
all those years, a litany
for the dead, or an aimless mantra
meant to cover dread –
that frame a gallows
where she had hung, a spider
strangling in its web.

The catch had rusted on the shutters
from disuse. She had to force it.
When she threw the shutters open
it was summer and the sun was high.
As her eyes adjusted to the brilliance
she saw the shape of things outside: a frieze
the wind set into motion, the fields
pouring like an ocean into distance,
the wind-stirred trees, the gate
like someone waiting, the winding road…

A knock came at the door and then repeated.
She threw the bolt to buy herself
the time she needed. When he had forced
the door, the room was empty and the loom
stood vacant by the open window.
The sun was blinding: the frame held
only light without an image.

It is not the business of another
to imagine any further. Once she has cut
the long threads of the story, its convenience –
she is free. Abuse *that* word at your peril,
it will return to mock you, like the nameless
who leave their names behind them –
the signatures that spell rebellion,
a freehand scrawl of bright graffiti
on the white, expensive wall.

Candied

In Eden it was never winter, the ground
stayed wet and spongy, the sun as yellow
and as overripe as Persian melon, the streams
gummed up with honey, and the apples mushy:
how things had got so soft is hard to say.
Maybe just being naked in the woods
with chigger bites around your ankles
and stinging flies and deep infections
breathed in every cut by rotting matter,
and, staring from the bushes, boars,
stiff-bristled, with tusks that tear
through skin and gristle – this kind of thing
would scarcely do for starters.

No, it had to be sweet
as grass, the kind of stuff that's habit-
forming, like all things half-conceived:
for instance, Adam
anesthetized, and God, part surgeon, part
cosmic dating service,
taking her out for the first time
to see how it would go (the Bible
leaves this part out,
although the Greeks, not believing
in premature withdrawal, left it in).

So I guess the way it ended was
that Eve got up, walked out
on Adam, their tacky Eden – sick
of honeysuckle, of trees stuck up
with signs to state their meaning,
and nothing to stick to your ribs

but apples – she'd had a bellyful
of those, an earful
of the chirping choir in the hedges, and
everything so blessed cheerful –
so she pushed past the flaming doorman,
headed out the road that unwound
like the wrappings of a mummy – that Eden
with its little sickly nightingales
the color of rancid butter, its flowers nodding
in continual agreement, its crickets and
its sticky, sticky rivers.

Concerto

I think of an early Christian
kicking off sandals and scratching, barefoot,
the shape of a fish in the sand.
And I think of the centuries passing, a long
torchlit procession down a corridor
of stone, lugging their armored dead, heavy
as the memory of Anchises on their backs.
And the outline of the fish effaced
by a passing wind, the earth bare dust
without an image, till at sea, miles out
from the jagged shadows
cast by the great cathedrals –
something leaps and makes a silver
bell sound in the sun...

this time, the little mermaid
waking from a fable with a start
has no desire for legs
to crawl up on the beach, to painfully
stand and walk the rough stones
to the castle, casting behind her
the wavering shadow of a fish.
This time she won't be standing
at the circle's edge to watch
the dancing figures: slim men in skintight
velvet, the women with their blossom
skirts that open as they turn;
out of her element, her new feet
raw, moving in her stockings
like live fish trapped in mesh.

Mayerling, Mayerling, the dancers turn
like figures on a German music box – a cunning
kind of verisimilitude, but wooden,
wooden: the music tinkling
like a shower of crystal in a hall of glass.
A picture in a fraying child's book,
its frame an etched black line, its caption:
"In the moonlit ballroom, how they danced."

Far down the beach, the fishermen
cast their nets; the sea pours through them.
She leaves her rock, the sun
behind her, dives back into her shadow
and as she parts the water, the long scar
of her leaving is healed in an instant.
At first, the gliding shapes are silent.
Though soon, as the legs
that she once longed for, grow
accustomed to their fusion,
as the shadowed lines along her ribs
begin to open like the slats
of a Venetian blind to let in water,
the silver scales descending with her,
she will begin to hear
the pizzicato of her sonar striking
minnows, the long strings of the bow waves
drawn across the bridges till they hum,
the wild choirs of whales singing,
the deep ground bass of ocean moving,
her own small waving tail the obbligato.

A Short History of Philosophy

We're here because we're here because we're here because...
CHILDREN'S BUS SONG, ORIGINALLY A WWI TRENCH SONG

One day the elephant gets up and lumbers
to the pool, looks down, recoils –
what is this lumpish thing he sees, this vast
and gray assemblage of loose skin, the wrinkled
knees, the sad eyes sunk in flesh like dough,
enormous horny feet, the limp hose hanging
where his nose should be? And what
are those crescent moons of bone that rise
on both sides of his jaws? He trumpets once,
sits down, and mud spills out around him.

He'd seen this monstrous thing before –
his mate, the herd, the great
gray clowns he'd traveled with, but he
was not like them – for he moved easy through
the bush, could feel the earth shake under him –
such power, and how he loved
to take the water in and fire his silver geyser
at the sun. And he had been
a mountain crossed with wind, a landscape
set in motion by a wish, and from the deep
recesses of his brain, in drought,
he could summon up by memory alone
rain forests with their varnished leaves,
water falling through the dark and shining
green, the red hibiscus blooming with a splash
as if in answer to the brass
insistence of his booming Gabriel voice.

And, though slow to anger, once aroused
he could turn the other creatures like a tide
that ebbed away from his enraged approach.
He was the one who moved, and moving, made
the world around him run. And those he lived
among, though their ugly bodies made him sad,
had always seemed the price he paid for company,
the way the old gods sought the mortals out
for sport, then grieved for them who were
so clumsy, quarrelsome, and had to die.

Now, as he sat mourning by the pond, he knew
himself their kind, a huge and monstrous
clod of sodden mud. He cursed his great
remembering mind – a Plato by the water hole,
descended from a great idea. And lost
in misery there, he hardly felt
the great net when it dropped, was
too absorbed to struggle when it caught
and he was hauled by derricks to the waiting
truck. And later he was taught to walk
by rote the little circus ring, to gather
all his weight upon a red upholstered stool
and turn while children laughed
and a lady in pink tights
made light of him by sitting in his trunk
as if it were a garden swing.

Sometimes late at night, he would look up
through the black slats of the boxcar
as it swayed and bounced along the tracks
and see the stars wink on and off, tilting
in the crazy sky that seemed so fugitive
as if, like him, it would fly toward a pond
in some lost forest in a greener world

and there, in silence, would look down
on a patch of stars at rest below, attended by
a swaying grace, gray matter, beautiful
as mind made flesh – at home
at last and looking up
from the quiet waters of the earth.

The Fourth David

FOR BOB, WHO GAVE ME THE POEM

1. DONATELLO 1430–32: 62¼"

He stands there sleek and calm
and dark in bronze, hardly more
than a boy, his stomach muscles
not yet hard. His poise is slightly
coy; he rests his left foot
on the fallen head as if it were
a hummock in the lawn, overgrown
with matted grass. Relaxed, withdrawn,
his flesh a speaking bronze, denies
base metal, says instead, but softly:
"please" and promises a pleasure
in its ease. His knees are slightly
bent, his hat is insolent, one soft
hand holds a stone as useless
as a flower; his sword might be
a Hermes wand. Shape-changer,
cool as the poplar's shade
at the crossroads, he stands
above his shield as if he had no need
of it – nude, indolent as May
that ushers in a lassitude
the young have when they only dream
of fame. His name is David;
he wears it lightly as the air
wears dawn. His hair hangs loose,
as careless as men are before
they know how they arouse
the giant, out there,
drowsing naked in the sun.

II. MICHELANGELO 1501–4: 13′5″

And now he feels the weight
of stone. His body, older, has grown
muscular and tense; he broods
the consequence of playing out
a part he never wanted, he who loves
the lyre and the lamb. He is enormous
in his sex, as if his power
were boulder-born, quarried by a hand
whose veins were throbbing with
a blood they barely could contain,
as if to act were risking floods
of red whose flow would make a river
meager. His pride demands
more than his heart can bear, Hamlet
standing in the hall by a tree stump
like an auger; doubt worms its way
across his brow and furrows it –
a freshly harrowed field
uncertain of its crop. He is a giant
who knows the power he holds in his hand
is only his until
he lets the stone go from the sling.

III. BERNINI 1623: LIFE-SIZE

Stand back. The time is past
all hesitation. His eye is fixed: the enemy
is in its center – out there, in the space
he wants to enter; behind him you can hear
the awful anthems and the armies crowding out the light.
His face too set and sharp, too hard
to be a boy's; his sex is draped, his body
shaped now for a different use:

to loose the stone is all, his will
is stone, the figure poised to follow.
The sling is stretched, the rock
is in his hand, his body twisted with
the torsion of the throw.
All his force is focused on tomorrow's
crown; nothing will stop him now.
Intolerable to watch
the slow unfolding of the marble
arms and feel already in your bones
the body of the giant toppling
like a forest through the years
until it's sprawled out on a field
from which the shade's been hacked, the limbs
and trunk from which the leafy head
is missing – discarded weight
that once set matter into motion
and dreamed a ceiling with an infinite recession
of heavy angels toward a filmy light like God.

IV. Anonymous 1979

Bronze will not soon speak again
in such sweet tones, nor stone relent
before the sculptor's hand.
How long ago it seems, just past
the flood, the last surviving pair
obeyed the oracle of Themis and restored
the human form by throwing the bones
of earth, the stones, behind them
as they crossed the desolate and flood-torn
plain. And stone grew warm and turned
to flesh, its veins began to pulse
with life, and only something flinty
in the heart retained the memory

of stone, that David loosed –
dead aim, the king who set the stone
in history's sling, and time's
the long slow transit back to granite.

At the museum gate, mute pipes of iron
stand against the sky. Beside them,
on a shaft ten stories tall,
a mobile made of burnished steel
turns in the wind, and turns again
in the dark mirror of the museum wall.
A child, call him David,
plays nearby in the sand. He looks up once
at the towering iron art, these giants
of an alien design, and turns away
and takes his mother's hand
and says, in a voice too small for anyone
but her to understand, "Now
can we go home?"

See-Saw

Somewhere the balance shifts,
world's end that hung in air, in ozone
mist, begins to grow in weight;
the little puffed-up self goes up
almost like smoke, the earth
comes down on the other side
like rain. These are the gravities
of change, an apple dropped
into a pond, breaking the surface image
there, where all the self-regarding
kept their face.

Back then, the earth
seemed weightless in the air, an empty
sort of sphere, glimpsed by the rockets
as they soared, a crystal ball
that held the future, like an emerald seed, inside.

While, Cyclops on a stick, the telescope
of every private Palomar turned back
on itself and saw
a huge eye staring up, an eye
as red as Mars, as merciless.
Like a volcano in reverse, it drew
the whole world, flowing, to its cone –
a funnel that made everything go small
in passing through. And nothing
was enough – so great its appetite, so great
its gift for shrinking what it fed on.
It made the world into a crater; one look
could turn the sweetest flesh to stone.

And then, by laws as yet unstudied,
the eye began its slow dissolve
to grief – such rain
that all the stones began
to steam, the oldest tale retold,
the deluge with a different theme:
no wrathful God who chose one out
and drowned the rest, but *Shekhinah*
who wept for what was not and saved
the living with Her tears. And water-fed,
the crops came back, the earth began
to put on weight, the trees rose up
like steeples to the sky and birds came down
to feed and sing the summer into grass.
And over all, the arch of sun through rain,
the sign of healing sorrow
Shekhinah
whose covenant asks nothing
of tomorrow.

So Quietly the World

I'm Nobody, Who are you?

Let them who love their names
in light, remember –
the journey into hell, the meeting
with the faceless, bandaged women
in the infirmary on the outskirts
of Saigon, Hiroshima: hands
reaching out to catch your skirt, then
through those flame-lit corridors
that turn and narrow, you
burn, the torch in the dream to light
your way back to the living...

sit down
the way the British Navy captain did, on the edge
of his bed in Bedlam, recovering
from psychosis, saying
his own name over and over
to end the nightmare
of the battle flares, too much
illumination –

as you say yours: anonymous,
not made to be the enemy of
man, not made to take
his name, but being one
who sheds
his fame, his self-important
naming, to state your own
unfinished, small, specific
business, so quietly the world
can still be heard

saying itself forever
over, like a prayer
the wind says as it turns
the birch leaves over, silver
or the light stir
of the dust
that goes on dancing
long after the feet that raised it
have gone by.

Ars Poetica

They wanted from us
loud despairs, ear-
splitting syntactical tricks, our guts
hung up to the light, privacy
dusted off and displayed, in ways
elliptical and clever, or
in a froth of spleen – details
of the damages, musings on divorce,
ashtrays from motels: films shot
on location, life made almost real
by its private dislocations. This
they said, was the true
grit, the way it is, no lies, the heart
laid open as a pancake griddle to the awful
heat of rage, rage and desire, coiled beneath
and glowing, until even a drop of sweat
or ink, let fall in its vicinity,
would sizzle. And over all, the big I
swollen like a jellyfish, quivering
and venomous. These things were
our imperative: the poet
in his stained T-shirt, all gripes
and belly, and, well, so *personable* –
my god, so like ourselves!
Oh yes, the women poets too, so
unashamed, ripping off their masks
like nylon stockings.

And all the time, the shy and shapely
mind, like some Eurydice, wanders –
darkened by veils, a shade
with measured footsteps. So many things are gone
and the end of the world looms
like a shark's fin on the flats of our horizon.
Fatigue sets in, and the wind rises.
The door is swinging on its hinges – the room
pried open, the one upstairs in Bluebeard's castle.
They have been hanging there a long time
in their bridal dresses, from hooks,
by their own long hair.
The wind that makes them sway until
they seem almost alive
is like the rush of our compassion.
Yes, now we remember them all
and the sea with its unchanging heaving – a grief
as deep and as dactylic as the voice of Homer,
and, as we turn another way, we lay the past out
on Achilles' shield, abandon it to earth,
our common ground – the bridal hope, its murder,
the old, old story, perpetual
as caring: the scant human store
that is so strangely self-restoring
and whose sufficiency
is our continual surprise.

II.

Meditation on the WEN-FU

When the Heavenly Arrow is at its fleetest and sharpest,
what confusion is there that cannot be brought to order?

Lu Chi speaks of the heavenly arrow
and the sky parts. Quietly: not
with the flourish of trumpets, nor
with the clang of bronze doors thrown back, nor
with the velvet pomp of the lifting curtain – but
with the almost invisible shift of a cloud
that had obscured the sun, or the way
the dusk melts slowly into dark
and the stars ignite. This is not
the firing of the arrow, but merely
the drawing of heaven's bow.

It is hard to draw, and harder yet to say.
For this the brush had to be
invented, to speak in a wet rush like the living
tongue, moving over everything as a stream licks over
stones, in love with the feel of what
is opposite, or meeting another stream
with the lush music of affinity, or
after a long coursing through the rock beneath
the earth, it cries up
into the light, as a fountain.
As to the flowing and the not-flowing,
no one can explain it: how the spring
that gentled the earth with moss
and drew from it the delicacy of ferns
suddenly dries up
as if the voice of a god were stilled.

And the dead ferns rasp brittle underfoot,
the dry moss answers the hand with the scratch of briars,
making it a place now for the tourist,
for the disappointment of cameras. Though,
now and then, one comes who imagines
she hears in the sighing of wind in the dry weeds
some spirit released – a bird sprung from a trap.

While, in some unmarked spot, sacred
to no tribe – a trickle begins in the rocks, and,
in the slow way vision alters from below,
a pool takes shape like a quiet eye
to hold the heavens in its gaze, the sky
looking up through floating leaves,
having found its proper home.

And, as to the heavenly arrow
of which Lu Chi speaks – it must have struck
straight down, deep into stone, into the heart
of granite. Strange, then,
what wells up, what pours forth in a flood,
should be both clear and bright
as water, heavy and dark as blood;
that stone be wounded into speech
and that such wounds should heal us.

Hunting Manual

The unicorn is an easy prey: its horn
in the maiden's lap is an obvious
twist, a tamed figure – like the hawk
that once roamed free, but sits now, fat and hooded,
squawking on the hunter's wrist. It's easy
to catch what no longer captures
the mind, long since woven in,
a faded tapestry on a crumbling wall
made by the women who wore keys
at their waists and in their sleep came
hot dreams of wounded knights left bleeding
in their care, who would wake the next morning
groaning from the leftover lance in the groin,
look up into the round blond face beaming down
at them thinking "mine," and say: "angel."
Such beasts are easy to catch; their dreams
betray them. But the hard prey is the one
that won't come bidden.

By these signs you will know it:
when you lift your lure
out of the water, the long plastic line
will be missing its end: the lure and the hook
will be gone, and the line will swing free
in the air, so light it will be without
bait or its cunning
sharp curl of silver. Or when you pull
your net from the stream, it will be eaten
as if by acid, its fine mesh sodden shreds.

Or when you go at dawn to check your traps,
their great metal jaws will be wrenched

open, the teeth blunt with rust
as if they had lain for years in the rain.
Or when the thunderstorm suddenly breaks
in the summer, next morning
the computer's memory will be blank.

Look then for the blank card, the sprung trap,
the net's dissolve, the unburdened
line that swings free in the air.
There. By day, go empty-handed to the hunt
and come home the same way
in the dark.

Metamorphoses at a College for Women

FOR BROOKE PEIRCE

For years he had been staring at
a sea of girlish heads, bobbed hair
or pageboys sleek and turned under
as silk sheets on perfectly made
beds. They were, really, flawless
little Andromedas, chained to their
desks, taking notes and waiting
for a husband to come and rescue them.
Their smiles were melting, no stone
in their gaze. And the days passed
like the glazed landscapes on
a painted urn of porcelain, vaguely
Chinoise, a little out of any style.

He wasn't sure just when it was
he first saw it – perhaps
it was a tendril of hair
poking out of a smooth
wave, but suddenly it was
the way a wave curls just
before it breaks.
That's when he saw
the snakes he hadn't seen
before, twisting and
hissing at the fringes of his
vision – and he reached for his shield,
and thought: dear gods, not me.
There is more, after all,
than one kind of hero; there are those
who, after years of patiently looking,
when they suddenly see their luminous bronze

shield fill up with the face of
Medusa,
smile, put down the sword
and say: at last.

This time, when the dragon
slides out of the waves, belching
fire and girl crazy as ever,
there'll be no one chained waiting
at the rock for his dinner, no one
with a double-edged sword to dismember
those gorgeous, glowing coils –

    only a bright sheen on the water
    a tumbled shore, and walking along it,
    an avid reader of Ovid with his book,
    and stretched out on her blanket in the sun
    a longhaired woman idly writing
    taking her dictation
    from the wind.

The Literal = The Abstract: A Demonstration

After all those swerving arcs in air,
the dance of shadows like an answer
from the ground, and all the dear
extravagance of flight, its sheering off
into delighted sky, where disappearing birds
with feathered script will spell
their life in flourishes
across a naked heaven...

as if the birds weren't there
to animate the skies, to dive
beneath the solid transience
of the bridges, the joy of water
in its rush to scatter
their reflections, a river moving
with its unseen weeds and fish,
all the unstated, understood
by context, as deer
surmised by thickets, or planets
missing in the moment of conjunction...

you may live forever and not see
a dead bird plummet down the chute
of sky, unless you have
a hunter by your side, his rifle
with its crossed-hair sight
to catch ellipsis on the wing
and turn it to a lump of bleeding feathers
falling at the same speed as a stone
in the perfect vacuum of the sky,
an elevator falling in the mind
where gravity is just equations

and the flight of birds
is only air in hollow bones, a concept
grasped by putting out its eyes.

The sun will send the birds
like notes from silver flutes into the air;
the gun
return them in a straight line
to your feet – the perfect absence
of what is absolutely there.

The Oldest Desire

And one is One, free in the tearing wind.

A woman, destitute, and taking cover
under the marble arch of winter, a monument
to some forgotten, bloody victory:
imagine a cheering crowd of red-cheeked
burghers, watching while the manacled
troop by, in the usual rags
of the losing side. The leaves look so
today – old flags trodden underfoot.

Which is nature? The dim, retreating sun
that's lost another round, the shivering woman
muttering curses into her torn-off mittens
to keep her fingers warm? Or
the triumphant beauty of the ice
that silvers every pond and makes a filigree
of ferns and moss, rimed so artfully with
frost? It's cold, and nature's beauty
beggars nature. This constant casting off
of what has lost its hold, an insult
to those aching veins, half-clogged
with memory and regret, but carrying still
the living blood. If only they would stop
their cheering for the winners, stop
their staring. She's had enough of their
instructive nature – that blackboard where
the lecturing successful chalk their names.
The bootprints of a passing trapper –
the shallow graves for half a tribe of ants.
Her mind rejects the lesson. She thinks
about the fields around the house
where she remembers growing; some days

in winter when the ice had formed
its crust on top the snow and you could walk
for miles – light as you were – and leave
no track: the white as blank
behind you as before.

She wishes she were small again – so small,
a speck that could live crouched beneath a leaf,
unseen, all-seeing – a little bit of ticking life,
a sentient particle of dust, but bright: a spark
whose crumb of heat could set
a summer's worth of leaves
into a conflagration. And then,
oh then, how merry, and how warm –
the flames running red, licking like hell
over everything, set free in the tearing wind –
and never to be cold again, no, never.
Her fingers are red, they stiffen; the people
are staring again. But she's beyond them now, one
in a million dancing points of fire;
behind her, the blackened, burnt-out miles.

Elegy for a Writer

FOR JUDY

We met where people like us meet –
some seminar or other. She looked, at first,
all angles – like a drawing by a cubist,
hard lines that she preferred, the word
if it was raw, unsettled
as a country whose terrain is too forbidding
to invite the colonizers. She had no
small talk, and the man that year whom she
admired, she never spoke to. She had
the reticence of passion, the terror
of the early wounded, and the courage
of those who try to write their way
past repetition.
Of all her stories, I remember best
the one about the woman
who, as her love affair grew darker,
just this side of carnage, bought
yards and yards of yellow burlap
and hung it in the windows of her flat –
nothing fancy, but it changed the light.
However bleak, however stark
things were – I still can see her, on that
ladder, hanging bolts of yellow burlap
and challenging the odds.
She lived the next year in New York
and wrote for a cheap encyclopedia to eat
and spoke to no one. The job ran out at Z.
I saw her off to Europe; she said:
"I'm never going to live like this again."

When she came home, she moved and
took a lover, became a teacher, invited
friends for dinner – these simple things
for her were the invention
of the telegraph. And the daily sun
was always unexpected: it struck her
as it must have Noah, when the world
had gone, perhaps forever, in the rain.
And the dust that she ignored
to write her stories, played in the yellow
shafts of sun that hold the windows
up to the world outside. She wrote
another story: a mother, dying, calls her daughter
to her side, says: "Take care of your father."
The daughter takes her hand,
says "No!" in thunder,
in the best American tradition.

She died on the Arizona highways.
Her lover and I wept together, and like
a pair of thieves, crept into her apartment
to keep her journal and her stories
from her parents, from the hurt
of what was hers alone, that hard-won knowledge –
the outline of the trap that she had
sprung; that adamant, private
soul that she had salvaged
from the wreck. We met her parents at the airport;
they had her sleeping bag; we put it down between us.

Her father kept complaining
of the heat; he didn't like
anything we offered him to eat. He said
he hoped to find a life insurance policy
somewhere in her apartment, made out to him.

It had been a high-speed, head-on collision;
her mother said the trooper told her
that her daughter had died instantly, but that
her heart had gone on beating
long after she was dead. I put my hands
up to my ears, and said I didn't want to hear
that. I hear it yet, that great heart beating,
and sometimes walking down a street
I think I see her – black hair, or something
in the walk, or in the angle of the cheek –
I start to call and then remember.

I have her stories, the latest versions, with her
own in-hand corrections,
in a manila envelope with a rusted metal clasp.
She had no patience with my elegant evasions,
she was never one for words to gloss
the facts. She would have said: dead loss
and sat down then to write and make it
final. If things are wrong
it's up to us at least to get it down
and get it right.

My Mother's Portrait

FOR GERTRUDE SHERBY RAND 1913–1958

I.

Those sumptuous, lacquered oils, a renaissance
begun too late, too many years waiting
for the children to grow, a husband
to come home to dinner, the sheets waiting
to be folded, those monograms of silk
a shimmer in the cupboard.
There was the silver to be shined
and lined up in the china closet,
the socks to be rolled and stored,
dark cashmere fists, in drawers.
So many years of lining shelves, the blue gleam
of washable paper, the polish on exquisite
French provincial, the clock's enamel face
ticking to the wall.

So when the canvases began
to glow with color, it was already so late,
so many centuries since the brush
was trained to follow the eye exactly, the slightest
glimmer of candlelight on a velvet drape,
a touch of ochre to a flushed pink cheek
soon to be varnished over, the elaborate gilt-edged
frames waiting, piled gaping against
the studio walls. So many people wanted to be painted;
unconsciously she flattered them, enhanced
the faces that she saw
with hazel eyes perhaps a shade too loving.

II.

As the years, like brush strokes, built their patina
of early age, objects began to pile up
on the neat white space, became at last
a clutter: under the table, with its carved legs
and sculptured-marble top, cramped space
began to fill, dissembled order, came more and more
to a confusion of brushes held, like a bouquet,
in a cup of India brass. The Renoir lady smiled forever
in her summer wicker chair. The precious little girl
copied from the cover of the Sunday magazine,
defiant in mauve layers of gauze skirt, stood
with her black mary janes catching the broken light
like the skin of lacquered eels. The soft blur
of pastel children's faces…the smell of fixative.
Some teacher who had tried to coax a freer form
but failed, had left a canvas of his own, an exercise
in flight, an explosion of birds, the sharp yellow
of beaks in a flurry of white feathers.

But the work stayed real in the old way, each detail
lovingly rendered and attended to, more and more
details, too much to remember, piling up
to a Victorian crescendo – no place
to breathe, the smoky vistas disappeared,
the foreground grew until it blotted out
even the pale *sfumato* of horizon.

III.

Then her studio was empty, the paintings
portioned out to the remaining sisters.
And I don't know what happened to the half-squeezed
tubes of paint, the carefully cleaned brushes,

the little table with the marble top.
I don't know what happened to the years
it took the children to grow up in.
Nor how I could atone for that postponement,
those portraits piled up inside
like courtiers waiting
for an audience with an absent queen.

Sometimes I think for her that I continue –
break up the frames, disband the court, send home
the sycophants who want their likenesses enlarged,
announce, for her, an abdication…
and we go off together with our easels
to the open fields
where the birds wheel in the watercolor sky
and the crazy wheat walks blazing into autumn.

IV.

I've only made another picture, tinted
the old print of a dream. Another mother
for the gallery of loss, that wall.
I need an instrument more blunt –
a palette knife to scrape away
these longings, scrape through, be done
with portraiture, soft words like that.
Scrape, scrape away until the light pours through.

And I'd let go those painted Russian dolls
that keep repeating themselves, smaller
each time, these images diminished by
regression, until they're nothing
but an eyeless button.
The snail's path, the winding roads of pearl,
turn back until one day they're finished.

Then the snail has her house and must move,
silver, on. Silent, feeding
on the leaves that give her cover.

Sometimes loss unravels slowly over years,
the old cord, the shed skin of a snake.
Those tribes where the navel cord
is left out in the sun to dry,
the wound to heal in a pucker of rose.
And the snake enters the grass
that has no path, no line can follow.
The brush turns silently to underbrush.
Everything loved is lost and free
to go its way, no tracks,
no turning
back, *yisborach, v'yistabach, v'yispoar…*

Labyrinth

sila ersinarsinivdluge

You've lost the clue – somewhere
in the maze, the golden thread's
run out…and the air
is getting thick and grainy as old film,
filling with something foul and dank
as steam rising in the heat
from a heap of compost: the animal's lair
is just ahead, the thread's out,
you'll have to go it alone and chance
what's there. The walls have narrowed
to a channel, damp to the hands
that grope your way; the rank air
hangs against the stone, as if
the stone had hooks and held it.
You can't stay where you stand; in the dark
ahead you hear the snorting
and the dull report of hoofs
moved restlessly in place, and then
the corner's rounded. You feel it first
before you see it, and know you've found
the chamber. It is a widening in the stone
lit by a feeble light
that's lost its force from filtering
down the deep rock chimney
from the sky, a sky that's so remote
it's dwindled to this sickly glimmer.
The floor that opens out around you
is spread with straw, in places worn almost
to dust that rises from the ground
where something stamps and stumbles
in its place; the cloud obscures

its shape, postpones
the moment when you'll have to face it.

As a beast will suddenly stiffen at the scent
of someone unexpectedly about, there is
the silence of held breath, a slow settle
of the dust. Just so it appears, as if
a mist had risen and the moon come out.
You both stand frozen for a moment –
two pairs of eyes take hold
and widen, each to take the other in.

The beast is the color of turning cream,
slender with a fawn's grace, fragile
as gentleness grown old, its large eyes
soft with sorrow, its horns
are ivory candelabra, its worn flanks
scarred with roads like countryside
seen from the air. It neither shrinks back
nor approaches, but waits, as snow just fallen
waits for the wind to shape it to the land.
So, slowly you approach, extend your hand and
let the soft nose sniff it, then touch the velvet
muzzle as you touch a rose, wanting to know
its silk but not to bruise it. And then
you know, and turn to go, and hear the light foot-
falls that follow yours and never falter,
only pausing where you pause
as branching way leads on to way. Somewhere near
you hear the sound of dripping water, slow
and even over stone. You feel a nuzzle
at your shoulder, as if to say
this way, go on. So, sometimes led
and sometimes leading, you go until you feel
the air grow fresher, and there's a filament

of light, a slow unravel of gold
like a ray of sun as it passes through the water.
A moment later, the two of you step
blinking into the shining day.

We stood high above the tree line
where the glacier's edge, touched by sun,
becomes a maze of running streams,
a million veins of silver opened into summer.
We stood a long time there amazed
before we felt the bite of hunger and,
together with the sun, began
the long climb down.

Recovery

Hercules, his muscles useless now
as sculpture, puts down the giant
on the earth that he had strangled
in the air. And leaves him there for dead, going on
to enter legend, another weight lifter
with an inflated reputation, his cradle
with the strangled snakes still in it
in the attic with the toys he had outgrown.

Antaeus stirred, and groaned.
He gathered his limbs, like something
he had spilled, and slowly rose
and stood – as large as ever, his dew-soaked hair
rubbing the highest branches of the trees.
How many years he had been lying there
he didn't know, how many winters
laid their snow across his inert flesh
he had forgotten, the centuries
were like a dream that faded with his waking…
he shook his head as if to clear it – the birds took flight,
and the clouds parted. He felt the sun on the slopes
of his shoulders and his back, the earth still
under his feet. He had no name for what he felt,
though some of it was grief for the lost
years, for all that might have been
and might be yet. And he wept as giants weep
and water planets. In the rain he heard them
calling – the dead, or the children born
while he was waking. He seemed to hear his name
in the rustling of a thousand leaves:
Antaeus, Antaeus, Antaeus.

And even in the distant towns, on islands
where the freighters seldom call – they heard him
coming. Even the patients, numb
on the silver tables, stirred, and stillborn
babies opened their lungs and yelled.
Dumb oxen looked up from their grazing
and power lines hummed in the air.
Somewhere in space, its mission aborted,
a capsule and its crew made their reentry –
those, who when they thought themselves lost,
could only think to go off automatic, take control
and turn the dials to another setting – back
to the sweet and clouded curve of space
that shelters earth: as it grew
larger in their portholes, the glass
blazed blue, and soon they felt –
as infants must, the moment
before birth – the heave
of ocean under them
and under that,
the earth.

The Continuous is Broken, and Resumes

Adam made the world
stand still so he could name it: the woods
intelligible as thought expressed
in leaves, and when they would not stay
forever green, he took the fall
and turned its gold to parable. And the long slither
of the snake became his dread
uncoiling in the grass.
The rock was his fixed idea;
the creation, to continue, required
his attention. The seasons he made gods
and, as the storms announcing spring
tear limb from limb, the holy ground
was smirched with blood to breed
the soft uncurl of seedlings. This murder
he called Orpheus, Dionysus, Jesus. Man
set it going, his matins
made the sun come up; if he forgot to dance,
the rain grew stubborn. His sin
had such effect that it could blight
the earth, bring on eclipse, rot the fruit
before it ripened. The great god he created
walked among the tents, his sandals opened
fissures in the ground, his touch
made the hills smoke. When Adam slept
the world grew still, mute as a great
organ whose towering pipes require
a little pair of hands
to move the air in thunder.
And how he dreamed of closure: obsessed

with falling curtains, heroic couplets,
and the absolute chord of amens.

Now everywhere he walks, the world is mute.

When he has passed, the birds pick up the notes
where they had dropped them, the wind begins again
to call soft speech from the leaves,
and the deer, seeing the woods deserted
by all but the sea-green light,
walk out into the clearing.
And the ocean nearing the shore
heaves a sigh of relief
and a great shudder goes through the swells,
as when a wind lightly passes.
And the sun, as the earth turns by it,
writes its changing shadows on the land.
Everything speaks of itself:
the fireflies in their code of light –
short flashes, the long dark in between;
the sand, grain by grain, is a pure reiteration;
the earth takes up again its ceaseless
conversation, picking up where it left off –
as a stream, after the agitation of the rapids,
where it was interrupted by the rocks,
flows on again, lyrical
as laughter, with the sheer delight
that can't be called indifference,
without the least concern for whether
anyone is out there, listening.

The End of the Line

The mind reels –
you feel the limits of the skull
holding the whirling cosmos in a thought,
the marching legions of the dead on a single circuit,
the bundle of nerves in the stalk of the brain
holding, like a Trajan's column,
the whole history of the race
wound and twisted
on the reel –
and the catch gives way
as the line pays out
when a marlin hits it
with such velocity it smokes
and the weak hands helpless
you can only pray
the line won't snap
and the great fish, blue and miraculous
as always, won't split the ocean's skin
and dive –

we've followed it so far

up the winding way from the salt caverns
into the blinding day, walking the weary nomad path
behind the grinding jaws of sheep,
seeding the even rows of fields
to the foot of the great stone keeps
rising to cloud-eaten turrets, the red silk wedge
of flags, the spikes of spires
driven into the midday air,
and the slow fall of dust into the crannies
when grass pulls down the stones again,

and the backs of trees broken
for ships, the blue fin of Asia beckons,
the ocean opened: the new world entered
by mistake – the line keeps paying out
the enormous blue writhing at the end

                                        as distant as ever
                            then, knowing you'll never
reel it back, that only in myth does the great thread
return to the spool and the weaving resume –
there comes the temptation
to reach for the knife

and cut the smoking line: the end
of tension and the aching in the arms,
the strained attention
and the gaping blue of what is out there waiting.

There is quiet now and the sweet lapping
of waves, no more tormented
by the thrashing in their heart…
only the ordinary breeze, the gentle tug
of tides, the amber light of late sun,
and far out, farther than the eye can track
or tired mind imagine
something blue as midnight,
            more powerful than hope,
swims free of our thin, killing line –

        leaping and sporting
lifting the water into the light: weightless
    windblown spray, a flower opening
        into mist, a fountain playing
                for the sake
                    of play.

Ex Libris

By the stream, where the ground is soft
and gives, under the slightest pressure – even
the fly would leave its footprint here
and the paw of the shrew the crescent
of its claws like the strokes of a chisel
in clay; where the lightest chill, lighter
than the least rumor of winter, sets the reeds
to a kind of speaking, and a single drop of rain
leaves a crater to catch the first silver
glint of sun when the clouds slide away
from each other like two tired lovers,
and the light returns, pale, though brightened
by the last chapter of late autumn:
copper, rusted oak, gold aspen, and the red
pages of maple, the wind leafing through to the end
the annals of beech, the slim volumes
of birch, the elegant script of the ferns...

for the birds, it is all
notations for a coda, for the otter
an invitation to the river,
and for the deer – a dream
in which to disappear, light-footed
on the still open book of earth,
adding the marks of their passage,
adding it all in, waiting only
for the first thick flurry of snowflakes
for cover, soft cover that carries
no title, no name.

FROM *maya* (1979)

I.

Landing

It was a pure white cloud that hung there
in the blue, or a jellyfish on a waveless
sea, suspended high above us.
It seemed so effortless in its suspense,
perfectly out of time and out of place
like the ghost of moon in the sky
of a brilliant afternoon.
After a while it seemed to grow, and we
inferred that it was moving, drifting down –
though it seemed weightless, motionless,
one of those things that defy
the usual forces – gravity, and wind
and the almost imperceptible
pressure of the years. But it was coming
down.

 The blur of its outline slowly cleared:
it was scalloped at the lower edge, like a shell
or a child's drawing of a flower, detached
and floating, beauty simplified. That's when
we saw it had a man attached, suspended
from the center of the flower, a kind of human
stamen or a stem. We thought it was
a god, or heavenly seed, sent
to germinate the earth
with a gentler, nobler breed. It might be
someone with sunlit eyes and a mind of dawn.
We thought of falling to our knees.

So you can guess
the way we might have felt
when it landed in our field
with the hard thud of solid flesh

and the terrible flutter of the collapsing
lung of silk. He smelled of old sweat,
his uniform was torn, and he was tangled
in the ropes, hopelessly harnessed
to the white mirage that brought him down.
He had a wound in his chest, a red
flower that took its color from his heart.

We buried him that very day, just as he came
to us, in a uniform of soft brown
with an eagle embroidered on the sleeve,
its body made of careful gray stitches,
its eye a knot of gold. The motto
underneath had almost worn away.
Afterwards, for days, we saw
the huge white shape of silk shifting
in the weeds, like a pale moon
when the wind filled it, stranded,
searching in the aimless way
of unmoored things
for whatever human ballast gave
direction to their endless drift.

Epitaph

> Though only a girl,
> the first born of the Pharaoh,
> I was the first to die.

Young then,
we were bored already,
rouged pink as oleanders
on the palace grounds, petted
by the eunuchs, overfed
from gem-encrusted bowls, barren
with wealth, until the hours of the afternoon
seemed to outlast even
my grandmother's mummy, a perfect
little dried apricot
in a golden skin. We would paint
to pass the time, with delicate
brushes dipped in char
on clay, or on our own blank lids.
So it was that day we found him
wailing in the reeds, he seemed
a miracle to us, plucked
from the lotus by the ibis's beak,
the squalling seed of the sacred
Nile. He was permitted
as a toy; while I pretended play
I honed him like a sword.
For him, I was as polished and as perfect
as a pebble in a stutterer's mouth.
While the slaves' fans beat
incessantly as insect wings,
I taught him how to hate
this painted Pharaoh's tomb

this palace built of brick
and dung, and gilded like a poet's
tongue; these painted eyes.

Unstrung

Or set upon a golden bough to sing
To lords and ladies of Byzantium
Of what is past, or passing, or to come.

It was a jeweled tapestry:
cut rubies hung for fruit
from the trees; lilies sewn into the ground;
the eyes of the unicorn were pearl
his horn a twist of ivory
his mane a fringe of silk.
The lady was all brocade and lace
her feet impossibly small in scarlet stuff
a satin band around her waist
divided her neatly in two.
The moon was a cluster of seed pearls –
a silver pomegranate with the skin half-gone.
The toy dog's tongue was a shameless red
as if the blood had run into the thread
dyed beyond the possibility of death.
And the eye of the little bird
glittered more impatiently than gems;
it tried its beak on its own gold coat
that tied it to the branch – tore it
stitch by stitch, to shreds
and danced in its naked bones, fragile
as the structure of a dream, or the anatomy
of lace; its call, a drop of rain
sliding down a single silver wire.
It flew into the night – a stroke
or two of chalk wiped off a slate.

The clock strikes; the bony spire of the church
is a black splinter

in the dead white thumb of moon.
The mouse comes out to forage for its young
looks up and sees, with widening eyes
the bat, who cannot see
as it sinks its teeth in trembling fur
a face so like its own.

East of the Sun, West of the Moon

She wore the skins of animals,
laced-up boots, a bright babushka
on her head. Every well was full
of witches, and the bodies of men
cried murder, or sweet love.
Icicles hung from the barns
and when she sought her image
in the pond, the ice was blank.
The geese wore a necklace of
frost, and everything shimmered
in the timid sun. The shadows
of the branches were scribbled
on the snow. When she saw
old women, bent back, humping
down the road, she'd run for cover
in the glittering wood, where little birds
chattered like teeth.

    It was in such a season, near
a place with a Russian name, the village
gathered in a circle on the snow,
began the dance, slow at first,
boots pounding the frozen earth,
ermine clouds trimming the air.
    They had put her in the center
with the bear, the iron chain around his neck
biting deep in the brown fur.
The dance quickened as the sun
caught the tops of firs, the yellow burning
through the green. Looking up, she seemed to see
from the weedy bottom of a well.
And the world spun

in the sun and in the centrifuge
of clan – it was then
the bear broke loose. He rose
until he blotted out the light –
deep in his throat a sound
like the ice breaking up
in the bay outside St. Petersburg,
the thunder of the spring.

They hunted the bear for days,
but could make nothing of his broken
tracks that bent and doubled back,
and disappeared.
           The girl was a long time
healing. The slash from one wild claw
had slit her face from hair to chin.
When it closed, it seamed her face
with a rope of red; by fall
it was a slender line, indecipherable,
like the road where it vanishes in wood
and you have to turn around
to get back to the village
before dark.

Water Lace and White Eyes

and the mist rising
as the temperature climbs toward dawn.
It is nearly morning, nearly spring –
whispers between darkness and the light:
white clouds out of the mouth, sun
at the back of the mind.
The white-mailed fist loosens its grip
on the blue river; the birds circle
following the compass of their wings
to make a hollow nest of air.
At the far edge a sled appears,
the driver wrapped in furs, relics
of the hunt, his face hard
under the helmet of frost, a sculpture
for the wind to
whittle to a fine edge. The geese settle
on the inland floes, their beaks pry
into the filigree of water lace;
the bear's paw
dips and flashes in the rising sun.

Twin dogs halt the half-disordered
team, the driver frozen at the reins
a Cid in the armor of the frost
moored in the drifts, his eyes white –
burned out by the light that blazed
for days across the ice. One by one
the dogs lie down, their ears laid back
in the signal of alarm, their tongues
loll red among the white crags
of their teeth. They whine, harnessed
to the sledge of bones lashed tight in place

with leather thongs, runners deep
in the drifted snow. The sun leaks
red between the hills, the dogs
cower at the rising scent
of what their driver, thawing, has become.
Suddenly, they pull
toward the four corners
of the frozen earth, like some six-headed
sinewy beast, or snowflake changed
to flesh and fur, intent –
in the growing light and unrelenting reins –
on tearing itself apart:
dead center
in the Northern dawn.

Natural History

We thought our arms
were like the lowest branches
on the trees, that, reaching out,
prevent the top from growing, grazing stars.
For years, for centuries, we pruned away
the parts permitting touch. First the twigs,
compassionate with buds, then
the whole branch, scarring
the trunk where the sap oozed out, hardened
into amber. And the tops grew
high as spires, so tall you couldn't
hear the birds in them, and when
wind stirred the leaves, the rustle
was so distant – we thought it
angels. We were armless then
as torsos of ancient marble dug
from sunken ships and set
on pedestals, eloquent with loss, speaking
of an old perfection – some balance struck
between the chisel and the heart.

But lately, there is a tingling where
our fingers used to be: the bright
excruciating pain of blood
returning to the numb.

We are still trying out our stiff new
limbs, touching things the way
the blind read   the language
made   by puncturing
the page,   letting in
the light.

MAYA

The yogi sits on the burning rock, a drying skin
that has shed its snake. His beggar's bowl
is empty as a skull; the sky *nir-vana*, without the wind.
His eyes are waterless and shed
tears neither for the dead nor those
who drag themselves through doors
to start the daily round again.
He is vacant as the space between two stars.
He lets the lion claws of sun
rake him unopposed. Chameleons, mistaking him
for stone, stretch out on him to take the sun
and lose their color to his own.
And still he sits, transparent soul,
a blister on the earth's brown back.

The woman, says the holy man, can never
escape from *maya*; it grows in her like maggots
in tainted meat, and drives her from his holy ground.

She runs, down the grassy path by which she came;
her passage stirs the grass to dancing. *maya*
maya…as she goes down, the growth thickens
the green and tangled forest takes her in.
Her skin is like the fawn's – indelibly marked
with sun and shade: in safety, ornament;
in danger, camouflage. When she sinks down
among the twisted vines and sleeps,
the darkness gathers at the center
of her eyes, the pupil of the moon
under a covering of cloud. *maya, maya*…
everything is close to everything, the stars
hang among the woven branches of the trees,

the moon is a lantern overgrown with leaves.
The first light rises from the steaming
earth; a heron lifts his head, his long legs
reeds that awkwardly step
out of their roots and walk, as the sun
opens his great yellow eye and lowers
his gaze, veiled by the lashes of the ferns.
A fish with golden scales leaps
through the shadow of the woman
as she bends to drink.

maya, maya…this veil is my skin
that hides me from him
who sees nothing.

Knowing the Enemy

The sun strikes the whale's back;
he dives, until the sun is overcast
with tons of green. He knows himself
full-grown; the burden that he carried
in his belly like a stone, is gone;
he has given his Jonah back to God.

For years he carried him, under
the furrowed trenches of his brow
and felt him walk by day the caves
under the great hill of his back –
this memory, this earthbound being
he had been. Since he was small

this man-thing had been tangled in
the mangroves of his mind, burning
like swamp-fire, or the hated sun,
searing him who needed filtered light,
for whom the mist was heaven.
Such preferences are fate.

When, with a great heave, he disgorged
this image that distended him,
he found it strange
how puny his antagonist had grown –
a twin-tailed tadpole
flashing off in foam.

His silver geyser rises in the air;
the bad dreams disappear
like islands off his starboard flank.
He moves, huge, through his own mist,
oiled silver by the moon, arrowed
as St. Sebastian, bristling harpoons.

The Round Fish

with neither bones nor skin
swims in the green haze of a golden sea
shot through with sun that tangles
in the weeds, like the woven filaments
of tapestry. Playful, he skims the tops of waves
like a skipped stone; plumbs the green depths
not as a stone falls, but
as a swimmer dives for his own delight.
On a still night, when you think you see the moon
stare back at you from the surface of a pond,
it may not be a mere reflected light,
twice-removed from the sun – but the round fish
regarding you, as a man may stare intently
at a mirror, trying, through the too familiar face,
to catch a glimpse of someone half-perceived.
It is no trick of mirrors, no infinite regress
of self-regarding mind, but the round fish
regarding you, recovering his own.

I watched a man one night, by a stream,
transfixed by the round fish, until he broke
the water with his hand, wanting to scoop
it out, like some demented bear, all his cunning
in his paw. When he drew back his arm,
his hand was silver to the wrist.

That night I dreamed of swimming, far out
at sea, beyond the line of reefs, easy
as you swim in dreams. And the round fish
with neither bones nor skin
swam near, the sky blazed blue, the fish
was rainbow-hued, right before he disappeared.

Surprised, I saw a jut of land I hadn't seen before
and climbed ashore, following the tracks
the fish had left, which fit so strangely
with my own. The trail now is not so fresh,
harder to follow in the undergrowth; still
it was something to have been started on at all;
it hardly matters that, where the sea turns
into land and the growth thickens – you no longer know
the trail you take
from the one that you are making as you go.

A Comment on the Relevance of Modern Science to the Everyday Lives of the Larger Animals

When looking in a pool on a quiet day –
the water shows your face to you, but
this is no mythical event. You are no
Narcissus, rooted to the spot, passion
turning to yellow petals by the pond.
Reflections are a trick of light,
the same effect is possible
in the cheapest bathroom mirror.
However, with pools, when you toss a pebble
at your face, it will dissolve
like an old pudding; the light, after all,
requiring a placid surface
for untroubled imitation. This proves
not only that myths are old hat, but that
mimetic art is dead, we are all
a stone's throw from dissolution, and
other post-modern notions. Two things, however,
require comment: 1) three minutes after
your face shatters, and the ripples
in proverbial fashion, spread to the edges
of the known world – you will return, as whole
as ever, nearly symmetrical, if not
unshakable: a return to contend with.
2) When the bear bends over the pool
to drink, he sees a pair of huge
gossamer wings beating over his shoulders
and a pair of slender hairless arms
where his paws ought to be. This proves
that mimetic art is not dead, that bears,

when they are drinking, are poetically
inclined, and that the muses
still perform, damp with inspiration
at the occasional watering spot.

Renegade

You can watch the sky from here, a fabled tower
by the sea, while the gulls wheel,
see with a double eye – here, a silver flash
of fish, there, the gray unmoving
cliffs. You could stay for years – Tasso's
black queen of Ethiopia
locked in a turret by a jealous mate
staring at the murals of an alien myth
bearing a snow-white child to suit
a Christian sense of miracle.
                                        Or,
some night, when the jailers
are drugged with wine or
nodding on hashish – you could go
in a slow circle down the stairs
with a single lamp to throw your shadow
in your path; so, darkened by your own descent,
gain the beach, wade out until your skirts
are ruffled with the tide, the tower
a black finger held against the night –
an admonition to be still. You could make a sail
of your skirt, hoist it on a stolen craft, outrun
the storyteller's art and cheat the knights
clattering in their ill-joined iron suits
of a certain rescue. Then the singer in the court
who weaves more verses than the oak has leaves
would find his fingers fallen from the strings
the next line hanging in the air
    a vine the wind has torn from the wall.

        Listen, the foam is whispering;
far out at sea, the stormy petrel
like some charred spirit from a burnt-out hell
her wings spread wide, tries the freshening wind.

Iphigenia, Setting the Record Straight

The towers waited, shimmering just
beyond the edge of vision.
It was only a question
of wind, of the command of trade routes,
a narrow isthmus between two seas, possession
of the gold that men called Helen.
The oldest of adulteries: trade
and art. We were to wait
for the outcome, to see
if we would be the vassals of a king,
or the slaves of slaves.

They never found my grave, who was supposed
to fill their sails, like the skirts of women,
with her charms. Helen, as the second version goes,
had stayed at home; only the echo
of the rustle of her robes
went with Paris to the high-walled town. I
stayed with her to the end, this aunt of mine,
and friend, whose illness drove her husband out the door,
dull-witted Menelaus. When she died
the swans deserted the palace pool
and the torches flared dark
and fitfully. I did not stay for their return,
like that foolish Electra.

I hid in the shrine of Athena –
hearing her, nights, pace overhead
with an iron step, like the sound
of the bronze age ending. The old blind
singer in the forecourt
must have heard her too, but

unlike me, he had to make his living
from his song. She was often sleepless,
as gods will be, and the nights went slow
under her heel's heavy tread.
When she went to stay the arm of
great Achilles, to save my father
for my mother's knife –
I slipped away.

I have just been living, quiet, in this little village
on goats I keep for cheese and sell for wine, unknown –
the praise of me on every lip, the me
my father made up in his mind
and sacrificed for wind.

A Private Space

FOR STEPHANIE SUGIOKA

This is the space where
the question of beauty enters,
in soft slippers, decorous, even a little
obsequious, muted
as if by choice. She kneels with
her pot of steaming tea; as she pours,
the long black screen of hair
falls across her face.
She handles her limbs
as if they were porcelain. She is almost
perfect, except for the space,
the shadowed gap,
in her huge kimono sleeves.
A hint of silver flashes
in that dark, a sliver of moon
on a night in September, the silk
chrysanthemums nodding
like conspirators along the hem
of sky.

(The icon painters of a thousand years ago
always left a little space unfinished
somewhere in the work. It was the place,
they said, inviting to the soul –
where the singular could enter the design,
the ultimate intensity of a slight
intrusion.)

One silver stroke: her eyes opened wide
as ivory fans at the flick of a wrist.
The moon slips through the silk

wrappings of the clouds. Later
she would pass through the rooms,
through the lines of mourners, like light
through the elegant
black lacquered slats of blinds, slender
and bright
beyond suspicion.

Beyond the Second Landing

The stairs are winding up
beyond the first landing, over
the little nest of rooms
where the fledglings curl warm under
quilts, past the spacious attic room
where dust and the sun dance
in concert every afternoon, the motes
floating down as the stairs climb up
into the well of light, into the twisted branches
of the trees.
          Here, the footing gets
tricky, the spiral tightens but
the breathing is easier; everything
lightens. The cobwebs brush your face,
you break through clouds – the blue
astounds you.
          You are standing
on the second landing, cobalt
laced with light. There are no bearings
you can take; it is too bright
for stars, and the sun turns away
even a sidelong glance. You only know
how high you are from the birds
circling below like particles of dust
whirled in the light.
          The change
is imperceptible at first – the slightest shift
of air, the stairs grow strange
under your feet, the railing
slowly roughens like a branch
of coral lightly furred with green, soft
as the hair of the newly born, sweet

to the fingertips. The blue deepens
as you climb toward night, thickens
till it is too dense to tell
from sea; you pass like a needle
through deep velvet, threading your way
up until you reach
                            acorns of light
hung among the highest branches,
swaying easy in the wind.
                            Your hand
still reaching up, encounters nothing;
the elements themselves support you –
a boat scrapes on the beach. You make
the landing. The earth
you climbed so far to reach
is under your feet.

II.

Bailing Out – A Poem for the 1970s

Whose woods these are I think I know…

The landings had gone wrong; white silk,
like shrouds, covered the woods.
The trees had trapped the flimsy fabric
in their web – everywhere the harnessed bodies
hung – helpless, treading air
like water.
                    We thought to float down
easily – a simple thing
like coming home: feet first,
a welcome from the waiting fields,
a gentle fall in clover.

We hadn't counted on this
wilderness, the gusts of wind
that took us over; we were surprised
by the tenacity of branching wood,
its reach, and how impenetrable
the place we left, and thought we knew,
could be.
                    Sometimes now, as we sway, unwilling
pendulums that mark the time,
we still can dream
someone will come and cut us down.
There is nothing here but words, the calls
we try the dark with – hoping for a human
ear, response, a rescue party.
But all we hear is other
voices like our own, other bodies
tangled in the lines,
the repetition of a cry from every tree:

I can't help you, help me.

Closing Ceremonies for the Bicentennial

(AFTER VIETNAM)

It was a long fall, that particular
year – the leaves stayed full on the branch
a long time, as if they would be green
forever. Then they reddened slowly as
a blush on the cheeks of someone
slow to anger. When the winds came,
finally, with the icy snarl of winter,
the leaves all seemed to fall at once –
like the armies of a more romantic age,
line on line of uniform red, falling
on the first command to fire.

The woods filled up with red, and the lawns;
the snow came the same night
and covered them; all winter, change
was only the slow shifting
of the drifts, the deepening
and the attrition. When the spring thaw
came at last, the leaves
were too wet to scatter, were something between
what they had been and earth.

When we stumbled on the first
of the bodies in the woods, we found
the snow had kept it perfect. That lifelike
look, that posture of some endless patience
with the way things are; the eyes wide,
the lashes crusted over with white crystals.
Until the sun came out.

                      Now the spring air smells
in that lingering way of a house when

something's crawled into the walls and died there.
But there won't be any finding, no –
only something, once alive, is in there, slowly,
outside of our reach, unwinding.

Lament

All morning I have been reading poems
from Vietnam by veterans (the Latin, *veteranus*,
old) young men
stunned into a deadpan
diction, writing between clenched
teeth, the way words bypass tears, step over
bodies on the road gone down too far
for any turning back.
                              Step over,
we are standing at the edge:
"if you have a home in hell
and a farm in Vietnam, sell it
and go home."

The green bags are tagged and shipped;
the faithful Buddhist hearts are quiet
in their jars. The water buffalo
is standing, as he always stood, in the field
that will no longer fill a bowl of rice.
Why does he turn from us, so leisurely, as if
no one were here? And walk away
with plodding steps, unhurried –
his swaying haunches
growing larger with the distance,
his hoofs ringing like temple bells
on the once green earth
of Vietnam.

The Illuminator

Here in our room
the light slips through the fingers,
the window slits cut high in the stone
walls; there is no sound
but the small scratching
of the pens, the noiseless slide of the brush
across white parchment.

Here we work unceasing for the others
while they labor; we're here to – well,
to save them, so we're told: us, with our
itching habits, our little pots
of gilt and ultramarine – the blue
we've pressed from berries.
We are the scribes of the unacknowledged world,
illuminators of the book we torture
with profusion: with foliage, flowers, beasts and
saints in strange positions.

We seldom speak.
The windows are too high, and
then again too slender
for anything but sky. If we look up we see
only a rule of brilliant blue, and that's
the light we work by. We are the brothers
who confess each other, and so
we ought to know how little
humility is ours. We dream our patience
will reward us; we take our time.

Yesterday I went out to our garden
and saw up on the hill

a cross a peasant planted – was it
just last winter? – a simple cross
of wood he'd bound together with a piece of twine
to mark the place the earth had taken
what he had thought was his. It looked to me,
who spends my days illuminating letters,
like a T. But it was almost lost in foliage, a vine
had caught it with a tendril and obscured it
with the leaves; it was perplexed by
wildflowers, and nearly gone in green.

That's why I went tonight to see
that farmer – knocked on his door and said to him:
forgive me. He stared at me in dumb dismay
and shook because I seemed a holy man, and mad, to him –
a little man in a frayed robe, gold-spattered,
with paint stains on his fingers, apologizing
for what he couldn't know
had never mattered.

Instructions to Painters by Wang Wei, Eighth Century

Mist, the weather changing.
And clouds close in, covering the break
of day. The light will come with rain.

Men, small and ragged as torn flags,
flutter in the gray. The distant lines
of mountains are as indistinct
as eyebrows on the faces of the old.
The whispering dragon
of the brush…the mist it breathes
out on the page…the waves
that open till they're oceans.
Your eyes forget
the solid world: the bruises
of the rocks, the black strokes
of bamboo, your anxious cry
lost in the tumult of the waterfall.
The rain has begun in the mountains.

The distant water has no waves
but reaches up and touches
cloud. The vanishing point is
everywhere the brush moves
heavy with water, waving away
the object world, going gray
into the gray water – and we
are the little men running, running
from the dawn, the dawn that is coming after us,
the rising wave we can't outrun,
but can turn, at the last moment, to record
its magnificent lift, the tons of water
poised over us – as if
too beautiful to break.

Mt. Fuji and the Martial Arts

It was something flawless,
something about the mountain: perhaps it was
the way the cherry trees
in their spring whitening, echoed the snow
in its composure at the top. So to
confound the butterfly
with the drifting of a petal to the branch
was to make the perfect
error. Or to arrange a piece of earth, a stone
and stunted tree, was to have the planet
in a bowl. Or breaking waves arrested
at their peak, arabesques
of the cut wood, the perfectly inked
block. So when the sword is drawn
and lifted high above the head,
its vertical divides
the mountain neatly into halves.
When the sword falls, the mountain is whole
again, past understanding,
standing over
the sundered body at its feet.

Made by Hand

Out there,
the scene that won't compare
with one we thought to stumble on
unbidden, the hidden clearing
in a wood that deep
inside a book one day in childhood
we had been promised as
a secret garden: there, where
the invalid boy you weren't supposed
to cherish, got up and walked, and
words hung dark and ripe
as berries in their clusters
you only thought were shadows,
sweet to the tongue and
guarded by the spiders, spinning webs
without a thought
to their design; it was just
that silk came easy from their flesh,
outlined their swinging in the air
with silver. As our mothers
the makers of lace, their fingers
all eyes, their eyes clouding over
with years – in time
had lost all sight of their design
as they grew better
at its manufacture.

We could wish ourselves their fate
and not avert it – the subtlety
of snowflakes on the tongue
gone in the instant of their falling.
We could wish for
such perfection, such dissolving...

Thoughts of a Retired Diamond Cutter

Care, carefully chosen, even
more carefully marked – the dazed white stone,
glass of compression. One wrong move, one
slip of the chisel – pressure
improperly brought to bear,
a trembling hand, any
of a hundred miscalculations, and
splinters: the shattered chance
in a million – the perfect split.

Perhaps I am mistaken. Perhaps
the glitter is only dust
on the workbench, a trifle struck
by sun. Is it ordinary dust
that dazzles us or
some important failure: the intractable
reduced in that encounter
with intention, dancing now
in a beam of light falling through the window –
failed in all but its resistance
to design?

Laurels

Enormous, the upper brain
rests uneasy on its stalk, unsteady
as the infant head on its delicate stem.
The little ape of love
and appetite fastens its long, slim
fingers to the stem and climbs
toward the huge gray mass of clouds
where giants laugh, holding their
immense sides, their castles of stone
swaying on thin green stalks.

Why does the giant have
the small black glittering eyes
of the rhesus monkey?
And why does the little monkey-man
going hand over hand
up the earth-driven vine to the sky
have eyes as wide as mountain lakes, soft
as the down that grows under the tongues,
under the wings, of angels?

What was it started us
up the long green ladder to the stars?
Who took the blue dome of our days
and darkened it, punched it full of brilliant
holes, each one dangling a long gold filament
of light we try to climb as if to storm
the walls of heaven?

Who waits up there
at the top of our heads, like some evolutionary
dare, taunting us, turning away

from our decay, wanting our blood, pretending
not to share our hungers? Has visions like
the crystal clouds we breathe
when animal heat encounters winter air?

Begin again. It is morning and a time
for simple talk. Here, a little monkey-man
holds another against his furred and fragrant
breast, and the strange trees, with their
overbearing tops, heavy as the willow
in summer, in snow, bend down
and brush him with their hair, whispering
"little one, little one…"
and letting down, one by one, their leaves, or flakes of snow,
until his hair is white
and he is crowned with green.

Love Uncommanded

> ...the great globe itself,
> Yea, all which it inherit, shall dissolve...

Extraordinary. Our friends,
the skeptics, who are
ourselves, such an extravagance
of feints, the perfectly spun
glass, exquisite complications, saying
they know that they know nothing,
the oldest ruse. Let it go.
Say what you know.

For once, be rid of the urn
with beauty chased in half-relief, the urn
with the false bottom, the ancient goad
to thirst – the right word turned
exactly on itself. Say what you know.

The glass is raised,
the perfect globe in which
the saint's heart sat, preserved.
The edges of the relic curl
like the tips of starfish drying
or paper that the fire catches.
The air pours in, until it seems
that the invisible has won. A fact,
it is invaded. A moment, it is dust.
Undone – this dust
you leave to air, where
it will dance and light
will catch it in the ordinary way –

it will seem then, as it does now, as if
a burden had been lifted.
The way your hair spreads out around you
in the stream, when the stream
takes it, the way things
lose their weight
when they rest upon the waters.

Winter Garden

After all these years of hating
the first-person singular, the one rent
in the good fabric: the lost solar voice
that spoke like lightning on a summer night
when the air lowered over earth,
almost the heavy breath of God – refusing
to break into any kind of rain, that thick air
where every drop of sweat was one more
rise in the humidity, every wish another
frozen flash of light; and the flowers slowly
dried, their petals, singed
by the sun's forbidding
light, fell, one by one, onto the paths
where people walked alone or in
oppressive clusters, always hoping
for the hunter's gun to break
the thick bushes into birds – loving the sight
of scattered flight, birds tossed
out on the sky like rice
at a wedding no one wanted.

Now it is good to watch
the birds gathered on the ground
where the seed has spilled on the snow.
We feed them all in that companionable way
Greeks leave fresh water in the bottles placed
in little altars by the fields. We've left
the wide waters where the old ships
used to plow their furrows, lines
of worry to disturb
the serene brow of the sea.
The taste of salt from our own bright veins

closes the wound; we turn away
from tracing those unimportant scars,
those roads we used to walk like pilgrims
on the trail of an old injury:
mea culpa mea culpa   why me?   ringing
their dry antiphonies in the brain.

We leave our kites caught in the trees –
these scraps of an ancient entertainment,
an old foolishness about flight,
with strings attached – we leave them
to the mercies of
the rough branch, the tearing wind, the last
dissolve of rain.
And when jets streak the sky
with their melting trails of smoke,
we are glad to be down here,
safe from the silver bellies
of the air's metallic whales: down here
where the furrows in the garden will fuzz over soon
with green, vanish into the lush cover
we coax from what
we can no longer see: the lines
that grow green again, then
wonderfully, most wonderfully, are gone…

Bridge Passage: Variations on Two Scales

1. EVENING FLIGHT

for Bob

Shh, the light is whispering, soft, day's end.

And darkness comes again, another way: late, lingering
and long, leaves warmth as it replaces light –
as tenderness comes after
anger, turning away, a hand
touches your arm, twilight

a bright smear across a fading sky.

The wind is hushed; the birds becalmed out on the bay
begin to stir, first with a shudder
of feathers, then
a white churn of water
at their feet, then the steep climb
to where the sun just was –
a lantern disappearing into brush.

Fireflies…the sparks where dusk
is welded to the night; the wind
begins again, and dark eyes
open in the wood. You can hear
the trees breathing,

the flying squirrel stretched

for a moment in the space between
two branches and the owl:
a warm furred x floating in the sky

on wings of flesh, it skims the wide
and dizzy height, fearless as those

themselves unknown, who know the branch
is waiting on the other side.

II. LIFELINE

FOR SONIA SANCHEZ

The old bridges are down
that led this way, blown up.
We've had to improvise with bits
of rope, knots
from a thousand ends: a macramé of old,
entropic bonds – bell ropes, the bucket ropes
from wells long since gone dry,
the ropes the Brothers of Saint Francis wore
about their rough brown habits, as a sign.

Space stares at us above and from below; our loss
has built this swaying bridge across
the vacancy. Everything makes it
sway: wind, your weight, a passing flock
of birds, the earth's turning, even the whispering
dead that seem to issue from below
like steam from fissures in the distant
ground. Sometimes it seems a web, miraculous,
thrown by some solar spider in the blinding light
of noon: a promise to step out on, or a trap.
Though we remember knotting it, it seems
impossible, the work of other hands, or forces
whose weaving we comprise, but cannot map –
though we must now trust all our weight
to its design: a little band

with quaking legs, afraid to look
to either left or right, hand over hand across
this breathless space, the way that climbers
pick their way up rock, afraid to move until a hand
has found its purchase on the slope.
But we're not climbing any more, just inching
slow across this fragile, swaying line –
praying that the knots will hold.

Out here, the wind is strong, tossed
on a blanket of air, we're dizzy from
the wild arcs we're trying to cross on.
We cling like insects to a blade of grass, depending
on a line of green that bends
and will spring back the second
that they leave it. No going back.

Hand over hand,

                slow, don't look down.

Hand over hand,

                steady, keep your head   .

where your feet

                must go: step,

                        don't breathe

step

The space is wide. It might take days, or years,
to cross. This time, to put our fear inside

parentheses, we're forced to think
of what we'll find there on the other side.

Ah, so you thought we had a master
plan, had built this bridge with something large
in mind, some sure ambition waiting, Jerusalem –
beyond this great divide. No doubt you'd heard
of how the Spanish left a green land fat with sheep
for gold. How their mind's eye crossed the sea,
saw burnished towers, set sail with an impatience
only the wind could fill, the ocean quench. The sun
set at perpetual noon. Well, we are a kind of sunburned
Spain, disabused of gold, wearing
the bright blankets of the tribes
who died in our tracks.

We go the way of birds
who migrate by the sound of tides
pulling at the continents as they fly,
who keep returning to a nesting place
where the grass is long, the cover good,
the broken shells attest
the long success of generation.
Some will leave their eggs there, others – bones.
If we can pass this space, this wilderness we cleared
in our first crossing. Now, in the last cat's cradle
we could string, we're trying to go home.
But the wind decides.

Meanwhile, swaying in the gray
air, we pick our way
and dream the earth
we left behind
is waiting
on the other side.

Notes

Up Against It

1. *"Trümmerfrauen* (The Rubble-Women)": This poem came from the description given by my friend Ingo Regier of his memories, as a young boy in Germany at the end of WWII, of passing these women on his way to school as they removed the old mortar from the rubble of the bombed city, preparing the stones to rebuild Germany.

2. "All the Wide Grin of Him": This poem, "...now I can go on and on," and "You, Failed Pronoun" were written as part of a *renshi*, a modern adaptation of an ancient Japanese linked poem, in which the last line of the previous poem becomes the title of the next. My *renshi* partners were Nell Altizer and Jean Toyama. "Her Body is Private" and "Of a Sun She Can Remember" were written in a *renshi* chain with Maria Benet, Susan Eisenberg and E. Alex Pierce; the latter was also in the chain with Babo Kamel and Carolyn West that produced "Judgment."

3. "What Was Going On" was one of the poems written during and inspired by the making of "Lilith," a dance work choreographed by Melanie Stewart, performed in Philadelphia and at the Edinburgh Festival by Melanie Stewart Dance.

4. "Facing into It": This poem for Larry Levis was never intended as an elegy. It was written several years before Larry's recent, untimely death.

5. "A Poem of Exile": In line four of the last stanza, the use of "jittering" for the uneasy motion of stars reflectd on open water is undoubtedly borrowed from the imagery of J.C. Todd in her evocative poem "Journal Entry, Carolina Sea Isle": "...Early stars / jittering on the surf like glints of fish."

6. "...Zero at the Bone": The field of burning moss has reference to the title poem in Marianne Boruch's recent book of poems, *Moss Burning* (Oberlin College Press, 1993).

7. This poem originated in response to a poem by Lee Sharkey.

8. "Winged Victory": The quotes from Cortés and other background information about the Spanish destruction of the ancient "new world" culture and its peoples comes from *American Holocaust*, David Stannard (Oxford University Press, 1992).

The description of the Sapporo Snow Festival is not the fantasy of an old peacenik, but an exact transcription of what I saw there.

9. "The Messenger" was inspired by the man with the orange hair. It was transformed into a dance work by Melanie Stewart Dance: choreographed by Melanie Stewart, music composed by Mick Rossi, with visual images by Jon Stark; danced by Tony

Agostinelli, Asimina Chremos, Kai Hinkey, Jerry Kraus, Paule Turner, Duchess, and Lea Yeager; performed at the Arts Bank, Philadelphia, 1996. A photograph of a moment in that dance appears on the cover of this book.

10. "Up Against It": The poem refers to one of the initiating events of the Spanish Civil War, the 1936 murder of the poet Federico García Lorca by Franco's fascist *falangistas* whose battle cry was *"¡Viva La Muerte!"* ("Long Live Death!").

There are several references to translated quotations from García Lorca: when asked what it was to be a poet, Lorca replied: *"Yo tengo un fuego en mis manos"* ("I have a fire in my hands"); a well-known poem of his begins with the line: *"Si muero, dejad el balcón abierto"* ("If I die, leave the balcony open").

Otherwise

1. "Night Fishing in the Sound": The echo of "cauldron of dawn" with Sylvia Plath's "cauldron of morning" at the end of "Ariel", was not intended, and may have been merely coincidental. But, if it is an echo, however subconscious, I acknowledge the debt. Context, as ever, alters the meaning absolutely.

2. "Being As I Was, How Could I Help...": The dance, "Cry Wolf," choreographed for Zero Moving by its founding director, Hellmut Gottschild, has been growing and changing over the years. It was its latest and most moving incarnation, performed in 1991, including a visual reference to the Lupercalian Wolf who suckled Romulus and Remus, that inspired this poem.

3. "When Asked to Lie Down on the Altar": This poem was written in immediate response to reading Marie Howe's poem "Isaac" in *The Good Thief* (Persea Books, 1988).

4. "...as soft and as pink as a nursery..." is from the lyrics to the song "The Girl That I Marry," sung in a booming bass by Howard Keel, a big beefy soporific movie star, in the film version of "Annie Get Your Gun."

5. "*Ume*: Plum": The pronunciation of *Ume* sounds the final e (oo-meh). *Sakura* means both cherry tree and cherry blossom. The emperor of the poem is the late Showa Emperor, in his 80s at the time of the poem's action.

6. "The Muse": The Lacan of this poem refers to a French theorist who has confused symbol-making with a certain part of the male anatomy. He, and his secondary and tertiary hordes of redactors, is currently enjoying a vogue in the Academy in the criticism and replacement of literature by a set of abstruse encoded signals, somewhat like those elaborately patterned clouds of smoke once reputed to have been sent through skillful flapping of blankets to distant members of one's tribe.

8. "The Lament of the Valkyrie": The line in the eighth stanza, "the crimson web of war," is from the refrain line of the poem "The Fatal Sisters" (1761), by the English poet Thomas Gray.

8. "The Secret Garden": This poem owes its existence to a story told me by Carlen Arnett about a man who thinks that women have a secret (possibly a secret garden), and they are keeping it from men.

9. "Those Who Come After" owes its precipitating thought to Mary Kinzie. We were speaking of the power of the Greek myths, still enlivening after all these centuries, when she suddenly cast herself into a future where a similar conversation might be taking place, and said, more or less in these words: "No one will ever say of us, what wonderful myths they had."

10. "What Was Left Over": This poem addresses itself to the poem by Sujata Bhatt, "What Happened to the Elephant?", in her book *Monkey Shadows* (Carcanet Press, 1991).

11. "Moonsnails" was born of my misreading of a poem by Susan Roney-O'Brien about mudsnails, which I took to be "moonsnails," that is, the snail-like silver patterns that moonlight makes on tidal pools. My poem rides on and then tries to recover from that mistake.

12. "Kazuko's Vision": The vision of this poem was told to me by Kazuko Terada, a former student in Tokyo, of an actual childhood experience, vividly recalled. What I did not expect was that in the retelling of it, it would form for me an image of the Japanese flag transformed into a little girl in a red snowsuit dreaming in a field of snow, which is how the experience of living in Japan humanized that emblem for me.

13. "American Painting, with Rain": The Sarah and Matthew of the poem are not just emblems: they are friends Sarah Lantz and Matthew Woodside whom I visited in Hawai'i. And Noah is the name of their small son.

SARAH'S CHOICE

1. "Never apologize for poetry" was something the critic Vernon Young said to me after a poetry reading during which I had abused the apologetic mode. His discussion of Robinson Jeffers's line, "I hate my verses," originally provoked this poem.

2. "Beauty and the Beast": The quotation, "These things in which we have seen ourselves and spoken" is from Richard Wilbur's great poem "Advice to a Prophet."

3. "High Noon at Los Alamos": The reference in "sentries set to watch / at Argos for the signal fire," is to the opening scene of *Agamemnon* by Aeschylus.

4. "The Towers of Silence": The source of the quotation in part III, "Stay with the body" (and the sense of it as the rock-bottom frontier ethic), is Joan Didion's essay, "On Morality," this passage in particular: "One of the promises we make to one another is that we will try to retrieve our casualties, try not to abandon our dead to the coyotes. If we have been taught to keep our promises...we stay with the body, or have bad dreams." In *Slouching toward Bethlehem* (Farrar, Straus & Giroux, 1968), p. 158.

5. "The Green Connection": The phrase "shine like pearls in water" is from Sam Hamill's indispensable translation of Lu Chi's *Wen Fu* (*The Art of Writing*), published by Milkweed Editions, 1991.

6. "Conversation with a Japanese Student": The word *akarui* is a compound word meaning "clear" and "bright." Generally used to refer to a fine day, its extended meaning denotes the bright time of peace and prosperity in Japan since the 1960s.

The quotation in that poem ("A beautiful and charming Female Floating Westward through the air, bearing on her forehead the Star of Empire") appeared in the text on the reverse side of *American Progress*, a popular allegorical print of 1873. The print shows Indians, horses, buffalo and bear ("on the left we find darkness, waste and confusion") fleeing before the various avatars of "Progress": frontier guide, hunter, farmer...pony express, wagon, railroad...cities, schools, churches ("The grand drama of Progress in the civilization, settlement and history of our own happy land"). The presiding white, diaphanous figure in the center is the "Female Floating Westward" of the original quotation. (Image and text appear in *The Incorporation of America: Culture and Society in the Gilded Age*, by Alan Trachtenberg [Hill and Wang, 1982].)

SHEKHINAH

Shekhinah: In Jewish theology, the Shekhinah was the merciful, in-dwelling (from the Hebrew verb *shakhan*, the act of dwelling), immanent and feminine aspect of the divine, a figure expunged from the canonical Bible, but who continued to live in various guises in the Talmudic, Midrashic, and mystic literature of the Jews.

1. "Emigration": The Mary Taylor who was Charlotte Bronte's friend closely resembles the figure in the poem, though I have taken two liberties with the facts. The original Mary Taylor emigrated, not to Australia, but to New Zealand. Since Taylor slant rhymes with Australia, I correct the record here and plead poetic license for the poem. The other divergence from fact results from literary biography's loss of interest in Mary Taylor after the date of her famous friend's death. No one much marks that in 1860, five years after Charlotte Bronte died, Mary Taylor returned to England at the age of forty-six. Nevertheless, for me, she goes on living "to a great old age" in "Australia," a rhyme in sense with the liberty her life embodies.

2. "Candied": This poem is heavily indebted to a delightful poem on a similar theme by my friend, Mary Hesky, whom I sorely miss.

3. "Concerto": Mayerling is the name of the hunting lodge where Prince Rudolph, last heir to the throne of the Austro-Hungarian Empire, committed double suicide with his 18-year-old lover.

4. "A Short History of Philosophy": A contributing source to this poem (which I realized only after I'd written it) is James Agee's last letter to Father Flye, a letter never mailed but found – stamped and addressed – on Agee's mantel after his death. The peculiarly affecting pathos of his elephant movie scenario stayed with me. The text can be found in *Letters of James Agee to Father Flye* (New York: George Braziller, 1962). Any resemblance of the elephant to Wallace Stevens is coincidental, though not purely so. The lines "He was the one who moved and, moving, made / the world around him run" are a travesty echo of the lines from Stevens's "The Idea of Order at Key West": "there never was a world for her / Except the one she sang and, singing, made."

5. "The Oldest Desire": The epigraph is the last line in Theodore Roethke's well-known poem "In a Dark Time," from his last book, *The Far Field*.

6. "Labyrinth": The epigraph, *sila ersinarsinivdluge*, comes from Joseph Campbell's *The Masks of God*; in this citation Campbell is quoting the Eskimo shaman Najagneq:

> *Silam* or *Silam inua*, "the inhabitant or soul of the universe," is never seen; its voice alone is heard. "All we know is that it has a gentle voice like a woman, a voice so fine and gentle that even children cannot become afraid. What it says is: *sila ersinarsinivdluge*, 'be not afraid of the universe.'"

MAYA

1. "Unstrung": The often quoted epigraph comprises the last three lines of "Sailing to Byzantium" by William Butler Yeats.

About the Author

ELEANOR RAND WILNER is the author of four previous books of poetry including *Otherwise, Sarah's Choice, Shekhinah* (all from the University of Chicago Press), and *maya* (University of Massachusetts Press), as well as a book on visionary imagination, *Gathering the Winds*, and a translation of Euripides' *Medea* (University of Pennsylvania Press). Her work appears in many anthologies, including *The Norton Anthology of Poetry 1996* and *Best Poems of 1990* (Collier/Macmillan). Her awards include a MacArthur Foundation Fellowship, the Juniper Prize, a Pushcart Prize, the Warren Fine Poetry Prize and Edward Stanley Award (*Prairie Schooner*), and grants from the National Endowment for the Arts and the Pennsylvania Council on the Arts. She holds a Ph.D. from Johns Hopkins University, and has taught at many colleges and universities. She teaches in the MFA Program for Writers at Warren Wilson College, and she is a Contributing Editor for *Calyx* and a lifelong activist for civil rights and peace.

Book design & composition by John D. Berry Design, using Adobe
PageMaker 6.0 on a Macintosh iivx and PageMaker 6.5 on a Power 120.
The type is Janson Text, a digital adaptation by Adrian Frutiger of the 17th-
century type of Hungarian punchcutter Nicholas Kis. Kis spent ten years
working in Amsterdam, and his type is one of the sturdy old-style typefaces
typical of Dutch printing of the period. In the 20th century, it was adapted
for hot-metal typesetting and widely used in fine books. The revived
typeface was called "Janson" because it was mistakenly attributed at first to
Anton Janson, a Dutch typographer who worked in Leipzig. Janson Text
maintains many of the idiosyncrasies of the original design and keeps its
legibility at text sizes.

Printed in the USA
CPSIA information can be obtained
at www.ICGtesting.com
JSHW020051290723
45417JS00001B/1